WALTER

I HOPE THIS MAY "
OF SOME BENEFIT TO YOU
AND NADC

MW01065524

System Buster

The Mystery of the Circle Revealed

Philip Beyer has created a
system of improvement that
is virtually unknown in
most businesses

PHILIP PAUL BEYER

Beyer Printing • Nashville, Tennessee

Published by:
Beyer Printing Inc.
1855 Air Lane Drive
Nashville, TN 37210
www.beyerprinting.com
info@beyerprinting.com

Cover and book design by Lisa Wysocky

All scripture references
New King James Version © 1982 Thomas Nelson

The Library of Congress Cataloging-in-Publication Data Applied For

Philip Paul Beyer, 1949
System Busters: The Mystery of the Circle Revealed/
Philip Paul Beyer.—1st ed.
p.   cm
0-9764822-0-7
1. Business I. Title
2005

Copyright 2005 by Philip P. Beyer

All Rights Reserved
including the right of reproduction in whole or in part in any form.

Printed in the United States of America
1 3 5 7 9 8 6 4 2

For information regarding special discounts for bulk sales

please contact the publisher at

info@beyerprinting.com

DEDICATION

To my father, Henry T. Beyer Jr.—a pastor and an evangelist for 50 years—who taught me how to manage as I watched him stretch the meager salary he made as pastor, that allowed him to support a wife and eight children. My father introduced me to the number one Book on my list of preferred reading. He also introduced me to the Author of that Book.

To my mother, Armellia Strimel Beyer, who not only taught, but demonstrated to me, the value of hard work, stewardship and serving others.

To my three sons . . . Paul, Barton and Brandon. Paul was our first paid employee when we started our business in 1988, and he has been a witness to every mountain and valley along the way. I pray that all my sons will continue to build upon what we have accomplished here that they might realize their own dreams.

And finally, to every one of you who hope to own a successful business; that this simple book might plant a seed that will help you to reap a harvest beyond anything you ever dreamed or imagined.

Except the Lord build the house they labor in vain that build it.
Psalms 127:1

ACKNOWLEDGMENTS

A very special thanks to Susan Meredith for her editing skills and encouragement in the writing of this book. I would also like to thank her for her poem "A View From My Window" printed in this book and which also hangs on the wall in our conference room.

This book is not for manufacturers only—
But for every business and organization
dedicated to achieving excellence!

Read on!

TABLE OF CONTENTS

INTRODUCTION

OVER THE PAST dozen years, I have had opportunity to see the power of industry and the efforts of many who attempted to harness that power—clash like Titans in an arena. I have seen my own early attempts and frustrations reflected in the faces of others who have dared to own their own business, only to find them stressed to the point of despair. It doesn't have to be that way!

My reason for writing this book is to show even the most ordinary person how to organize, build and grow an extraordinary business through a systematic approach. I didn't want to begin writing this book until I had tested the system myself. I wanted to see the systems actually work—to watch how they transform a company step-by-step. My hope now is to help others discover what I call "The Mystery of the Circle"—a *must* for building a successful business. More about that later!

We have been able to break down all facets of business systems that seem very complicated into something easy to understand. In fact, I will introduce in this book the very systems we have used to transform our company. Some are so simple, I'm still amazed that many organizations have not implemented, nor even discovered them. I have proved to myself that any person who is willing to put their shoulder to the wheel—and not look back—can build a successful organization that will serve, educate and stand for all that is great about America—a model of excellence for other businesses.

This book is for . . .

• Those who may not have a business education or training, but who have the drive and vision to launch their own business;

• Those who have already started a business and find themselves struggling day after day through what seems insurmountable chaos;

• Managers of small-to-large organizations and companies who want to improve their skills and see their company grow and prosper.

But for those of you who do have many years of business education and experience, I feel confident you will pick up a few priceless nuggets of fine gold. They were mined under extreme pressure!

I started my business in 1988. By 1993, I was experiencing major problems. According to the Small Business Administration, over 50 percent of small businesses fail in the first year and 95 percent fail within the first five years. A great many of these businesses fail in the fourth or fifth year because they have usually grown to a size where the owner can no longer maintain proper control.

In my fifth year, I realized I didn't own a business—it owned me! I only had a very difficult job. Most business problems come to the surface after growing to a certain size, and then the floodgates of chaos are opened. You find that your business is too big for you to keep all the information in your head, while you still do most of the work. And it's too small to hire the people you think you need to handle the chaos. As long as you are a one or two-person operation, everything goes rather smoothly. But when you get to four or more employees . . . WATCH OUT!

I have included many true stories and anecdotes in this book, because I believe they paint pictures that communicate complex ideas in a simple way. I worked literally thousands of hours for ten years, building a network of systems that I now call *System100* that can virtually systematize every aspect of an organization from top to bottom.

Over the last four or five years, many suggested I write a book on organization and systems. I assume they thought I had it all worked out even then and was some kind of "systems guru." But I believe unless you've actually completed something from start to finish, you really don't know how or *if* it will work. I also understood there was still a lot to learn even towards the end of completing a truly "turnkey" system. So, the time for a book had not yet arrived—there was still much left to do.

TURNKEY
Supplied, installed, or purchased in a condition
ready for immediate use, occupation, or operation

Not long ago, I was talking with an older salesman at the largest manufacturer of printing presses in the world. He told me the thing he had come away with, after years of visiting thousands of printing companies, is the wonder that anything ever gets through the printing process correctly. The greater wonder, for me—after countless meetings and discussions of my own with business people and leaders over the years—was that so many companies remain chaotic, and that for most businesses chaos is taken for "normal."

A close friend of mine said it like this: "A business without good systems is like a body without a central nervous system—lots of loose nerve ends reaching for something that doesn't exist." I call the operation of that kind of a company the *"Anti-System Solution."*

The mindset of the Anti-System Solution is that . . .

- Systems are for very large organizations only—or not necessary at all.
- You need good people—not good systems.
- More customers bringing in more money is the answer to our problems.

JUST IMAGINE!

If one of these Anti-System Solution companies were to be totally honest with its employees, they might send out a series of *Memos from Management* that read like the following:

MEMO: Due to lost customers, a powerful marketing campaign will be launched to bring in more business.

MEMO: Due to more chaos from these new customers, more meetings will be needed to deal with employee frustrations, production and service problems.

MEMO: Due to production and service problems, new managers are being hired to handle the chaos.

MEMO: Due to a lack of profits from soaring marketing costs and upper management costs, we need to reduce budgets in the following areas: Employees salaries, service maintenance and new equipment acquisitions.

MEMO: Due to a lack of skilled employees from budget cuts, more managers will be hired to fill in the gaps.

MEMO: Due to budget cuts for maintenance and new equipment, there are now more equipment breakdowns . . . which has created employee frustration . . . which is creating employee turnover . . . which is creating missed deadlines . . . which is also resulting in lost customers.

MEMO: Due to lost customers and red ink, a powerful marketing campaign will be launched to bring in more business. Also a NEW AND IMPROVED consultant will be brought on site to figure out what our problem is. P.S. Our consultant has asked us not to call what we are experiencing "problems" . . . but "opportunities."

Do You Know a Business That is Experiencing Those Kinds of "Opportunities?"

Bear hunting is an "opportunity." But at some point you need to stop and consider: Have you got the bear, or has the bear got you!?

Why is there in the hand of a fool the purchasing price of wisdom, since he has no heart for it?
Proverbs 17:16

A Day in the Life of Some American Businesses

Cranky opens his place of business in the morning at 8 o'clock, Bob gets there at 8:20, Sue and Mary get there at 8:45, and Jim gets there about 10:00. Bob and Sue answer the phones until Jim decides to show up, and then Cranky answers the phone when Sue goes to the bank. Now on Wednesday's, Sue can't go to the bank so Jim goes, but if he is on call then Mary can go, if she can borrow Cranky's car, because her teenage son takes it to school. Cranky takes care of doing payroll on Friday unless he is having lunch with a client; then Sue will do it. Jim takes in most of the job orders unless he is called to the shop to handle problems in production, and then Bob will take the orders. Bob doesn't like taking job orders, so sometimes he just lets the phone ring until Cranky answers the phone and takes the order. But when Cranky takes the job order he usually writes it up wrong, so Jim gets mad at Bob for not doing his job because Bob says his job is selling, and why should he have to take in orders. Cranky gets upset at Jim and Bob for quarreling and says if Bob is too *d#%* busy, then we will have Mary give us a hand, except on Wednesdays because she is working on getting the *d#%* invoices out for the week. So we will have Sue do it on Wednesday. Bob thinks, "What is Cranky's problem . . . what is he so upset about?" I think you get the point!

In commercial printing, the process from data entry to shipping is extremely complicated. Each job is custom, and the variables seem almost infinite. I guess, if you wanted to tackle something hard to organize and turnkey to the extent of the McDonald's Hamburger Corporation, it would be a printing company. In fact, when I first began to build *System100* to turn-key my company I was told by another printing company owner, "It can't be done, there are just too many variables." To tell you the truth, in my second year of building the system I started to believe I had taken on the impossible . . . but I pressed on!

You may have seen the circus performer who spins ceramic plates on a row of long poles. He puts a plate on a pole gives it a spin and moves on to the next pole and spins another plate and so on. Sometimes, as he is spinning a new plate, one of the first plates falls to the ground. So he runs back and puts on a new plate and gives it a spin. There is a point in the act where the performer is running up and down the row trying to keep all the plates spinning. He seems anxious and frantic for a time; but when he gets them all spinning, he is all smiles, because now all he has to do is walk up and down the row giving each plate a gentle tap with his finger to keep them all spinning merrily without falling off the poles.

This is how it will seem when you are setting up systems for your organization. Just when you think you have a system working well, it will crash. But you can't give up; you just pick it up and get the system operating again. It's not like you have to build the system from the ground up each time. You will appreciate, that once all your systems are up and running, you only have to tweak a system every now and then.

In my sixth year of building *System100*, I was receiving a lot of comments and questions from my customers and vendors about how clean and organized our company was. Some even asked me to speak to different groups of their employees on how we set up our systems and how we keep our building so clean and well organized. I honestly want to serve and to see my customers become more organized themselves, and I have found I really enjoy sharing what I have learned over the years, building the systems that transformed our company into one of excellence.

In 1998, I was thankful to have everything in the business and my personal life paid off. I could have gone fishing or golfing. My company operations manual was built, and my systems were working fine. But I felt there was something missing. I had the desire to own a really nice building for my business, and to take my systems to the people. I could have done like some consultants recommend . . . "sell when you get your company turn-keyed or franchise-ready." But I wanted to reach up to a higher level . . . give it my utmost . . . and ultimately teach others my systems through a book like the one you are holding. Beyond that, I wanted to develop a computer program that would contain all of these systems in a format that could be customized for virtually any kind of business or organization. It would have everything someone would need to start up or transform their business almost over night. *System100* is now available in that format.

It has been my desire to introduce serious business people to this new *System100* software program. It's easy to understand, can be quickly implemented—and you don't have to spend ten years building the 'mousetrap' yourself from the ground up.

This book, *System Buster: The Mystery of the Circle Revealed*, is able to show people with dreams of owning or successfully managing a business, a step-by-step method of how to do it—not just a philosophy and some rose-colored stories and illustrations about other successful companies. The book is also the beginning of a new venture that will launch ebizproducts.com.

What you will read here is a product of ten years of testing, re-testing and finally proving the systems that have transformed our company into one of turn-keyed excellence. You won't need a consultant to interpret this book . . . you can understand it easily for yourself.

Be aware! Setting out on this adventure, to *totally systemize your operation*, is not for the faint of heart. But I believe it will revolutionize your business and, quite possibly, your life.

Some people grow stronger assuming responsibilities;
others grow weaker doing nothing.
Henry T. Beyer Jr., Bread of Truth ©1997

CHAPTER 1
DAY OF DECISION

IN 1993, ONE of our regular customers stopped by my first small printing shop in Nashville, Tennessee to have some copies made. As we were having a casual conversation, I noticed he was eyeing the shop with a less than approving look on his face. He said, "Philip, you need to clean this place up, it looks awful, and it doesn't make a very good impression!"

I was pretty embarrassed, to say the least, and felt a little defensive. After he left, I wondered, "Who does he think he is, coming into my shop and telling me how to run my business?" The more I thought about it, the madder I got.

As I was thinking about what had just happened, I turned and looked up on the wall and there was the large, ragged-edged sign I had posted a year or so earlier. The sign simply read . . .

JOHN 3:16

You may be familiar with this Bible verse that states, "For God so loved the world, He gave His only begotten Son, that whosoever believes on Him should not perish, but have everlasting life." Well, at that very moment I had the distinct impression that God was saying to me, *"Philip, either put this place in order or take My name down. What the customer said to you is true!"*

Yes, my company was in chaos, my nerves were on edge, and I was dropping balls right and left. We were making a lot of mistakes in production—many orders were being taken and then misplaced. Customers would call and ask me about a job in progress and it might take me twenty minutes to find it. An old job order that was supposed to be filed would sometimes take hours to locate. The place was messy and disorganized. I had so many papers on my desk they were falling off on the floor. I couldn't leave the shop without my employees having major problems. I had to admit I really didn't know how to organize even a small company with only four or five employees. That's a terrible place to be: knowing there's a big problem, but not knowing how to correct it or where to begin!

An Answer Comes

A few weeks later one of my best friends, Van, came to the shop and noticed I was really stressed out. I was complaining about the mess and the fact that I couldn't keep up with it all. Van wasted no time in asking me to take a ride with him. I told him, "Van, I can't leave the shop, because every time I leave this place it costs me two hundred dollars in mistakes."

But Van wouldn't take "no" and pressed me to "Come on and take a ride. Besides you need to get out of here for a while. We'll be right back."

I finally agreed to go, but with a first-class attitude.

We ran an errand or got something to eat (I really don't remember), but on the way back to the shop I noticed he was taking a detour to his house. I was getting pretty irritated, and told him I didn't have time for that, but he said he'd only be a minute. When we pulled up to his house, he jumped out, ran inside, and came out a minute later with a book in his hand. He threw it on the front seat, and said, "Read this! It will help you with the shop."

Now he was getting on my last nerve! "I don't have time to read books," I barked. "I'm just too busy with the business and the rest of my life." But, I took the book home after work that day, and set it aside.

About two weeks later, I decided to read before going to sleep, and there laid Van's book: *The E-Myth* by Michael Gerber. Some title! What's the "E" stand for? I wondered negatively. But I began to read, and as I got into the second chapter, I swear I bolted straight up in the bed.

It was like a light had come on in my head. I said, "I know what to do! I know how we can fix this thing!" It was just a simple story in the book about a man going to a hotel and the great service he had received and how the hotel had a system to make that great service happen. Now, the book didn't tell me step-by-step how to fix or turnkey a printing company, but it gave me the spark needed to light the fire and the passion for a mission to fulfill the vision I believed God had placed in my heart.

All the years of being a self-employed entrepreneur came together with almost total understanding, in just a moment of time. I set out to find other books and tapes; and the counsel of other business owners. I read everything I could put my hands on to help me prepare for the work ahead. I was going to turn the vision into reality, and turn Beyer Printing into its utmost . . . for His Highest. And I couldn't wait to get started.

In the day of my trouble I will call upon You,
For You will answer me.
Psalms 86:7

CHAPTER 2
BEGINNING THE MISSION

Facing this challenge head-on, I thought it was time to take a good hard look at my own life.

Do I really seek truth or do I avoid things I don't want to deal with? Do I procrastinate and sweep things under the carpet? As an entrepreneur, do I jump from one project or business idea to the next, never totally completing anything? Do I really dot the I's and cross the T's? Or do I approach things haphazardly, saying to myself it's not that important or it's so small no one will ever notice?

There's a story about Michelangelo the painter . . . that one day his employer, who had commissioned him to paint the Sistine Chapel, noticed Michelangelo spending a significant amount of time in one dark corner of the building. He asked Michelangelo why he was being so meticulous when no one would see it? Michelangelo simply said, "God sees!"

Well, you may not think that's reason enough to do your best in all situations, but what I will reveal in this book will explain in detail the reasons you should.

Do I Need a Consultant?

Companies that are just starting out, those experiencing trouble, and owner/managers who find themselves overwhelmed and weary,

often turn to motivational seminars to find answers. You will hear
the fine-sounding words of some who seem to have the cure for all
your ills. Proverbs 15:22 reads: "Without counsel, plans go awry,
but in the multitude of counselors they are established." Wisdom
says we need to keep our ears open to *good* counsel. But here's
where discernment is needed.

There are some exceptionally motivating speakers on the "circuit," but there are also thousands of self-proclaimed "gurus"—I call
them the "Rah Rah" boys—who (if "busted") would prove to be less
than the experts they make the big bucks to imitate. Beware of those
who would move into your operation, make themselves "invaluable" . . . and then bleed you dry. If an "expert" does not have the
heart to serve your best interests, and to see your company prosper
without draining or taxing its resources, I would look elsewhere. In
fact, I would recommend you run for your life!

As I contemplated writing this book, a friend of mine brought
me the cartoons below. Not only are they funny, they are also sadly
true.

Printed by permission:

Dilbert by Scott Adams

A lot of consultants (Consul*ticks*) give you systems only *they* can understand. They actually become part of the system they will charge you to put in place. They will expect you to rely on their "expertise" for your success. Yes, they want to become part of you—and you can't remove them without leaving a large hole in your side.

The two most important questions these people could answer for you are: Have you done it? And, have you actually, successfully built a company from the ground up and seen it thrive?

I believe whole-heartedly, that if you will continue reading this book and implement the things that apply to your organization, you can build an excellent system—and possibly a world-class operation—without me or any Consul*tick.*

You know the old adage, "Give a hungry person a fish to eat and tomorrow they will need another fish, but give them a fishing pole and teach them to fish and they can feed themselves."

> *Confidence in an unfaithful man in time of trouble*
> *is like a broken tooth, and a foot out of joint.*
> Proverbs 25:19

So, What is Truth?

I decided I would seek the *truth*, whatever the cost . . .

I would demand the truth from my employees and myself.

I would not accept office politics in place of truth.

I would leave no stone uncovered.

I would continually improve the company through a systematic approach in every area of the business, even as detailed as a paper clip out of its place.

I would continue my education on business and keep up with the latest technology, but I would refuse to be sidetracked with the latest trends or fads in the business world.

I made a promise to God that I would not start on another business venture that might take me away from my mission until my company was completely turn-keyed and reflected His excellence.

I had no idea how long it would take. And, I guess, if you had told me then that it would take ten years, I might not have made the journey. But I knew if I was going to commit to this . . .

It All Had to Start With Me—And I Would Have to Change!

If you look at the books I recommend reading on page 130, you will see the Bible tops the list. The reason I have it at the top is that, through my research, I have discovered that most principles and philosophies found in the celebrated business books of our time, can be directly traced to the Bible—just like the founding documents of the United States that also have their roots in the Bible.

I'm sure you've heard it said, "The truth will set you free!" Well, I've learned in business and in my life that is absolutely true. Only when you know the truth about an issue or problem, can you *fix* it. If you don't believe in this concept, I suggest you put this book down, because from here I only go deeper into the truth—and it will cost you. But I'm here to tell you it's well worth it!

For which of you, intending to build a tower, does not sit down first and count the cost, whether he has enough to finish it—lest, after he has laid the foundation, and is not able to finish, all who see it begin to mock him, saying, This man began to build and was not able to.
Luke 14:28-30

CHAPTER 3
WRITING IT ALL DOWN

THE NIGHT I got the vision for how to fix what was wrong with my company, I knew I needed to write it all down, so I could refer back to it:

- How do I want my company to look?
- How should my employees and I conduct ourselves?
- What is the importance of quality and service to me and to my customers?

I even made a list of character traits that I thought would make a great employee and an owner. I called it *Profile of the Ideal Employee*. See page 123. You may want to add to my list.

I also wrote down how I wanted this new company to conduct itself as far as morals and integrity. See our *Code of Ethics* on page 125.

The Ten Commandments, our Constitution and The Bill of Rights are all written documents used as guides to build lives and a nation. A mission statement, along with many other supporting documents, can be used as a guide to build a great company. Each added document should build upon the mission statement; not drift away from it. See our *Mission Statement* on page 124.

A Written Document Keeps You on Course

The Constitution of the United States says that all men are created equal. And yet, at the time it was written you and I both know there was slavery in the United States. Does this mean that the Constitution is of no use? Since the founding fathers were not totally living up to its standards, does that mean we should abandon it? God forbid! Can't you see that the Constitution was a vision for a great nation, written down by men? But it takes a long time to fulfill a great vision. We keep going back to the Constitution as our guide.

Fredrick Douglas, the black orator during the Civil War, used the Constitution's great words and ideals to hold our government accountable, saying, "See? You are not living up to your own words in your own written document." It still guides our government today and points out whether our laws are on course. Our courts and judges measure our laws against these founding documents. That's why we hear people ask if this or that law is Constitutional, or not. All other laws we might implement are measured against the measuring stick we call The United States Constitution—the most workable system a nation ever put in place.

Your company's mission statement and code of ethics can act as your founding documents; your "Constitution." All of your policies should measure up against it. Constitution actually means establishment or laying the foundation. You've heard the term, *He has a strong constitution.*" Thank God, our country takes our mission statement—the Constitution—seriously!

Everything in your company's written system—your operations manual—should strengthen your mission statement. *A mission statement can become mere words on a piece of paper or it can become a living document guiding you through the years of building a great company or organization.*

I remember one time I called the company of an author of one of the books you'll find on my recommended list, and I was put directly into general delivery voice mail. I thought to myself, "This guy is so systematic, I'll bet I will hear back from him immediately." But a week went by and no return phone call. I decided this must be a fluke, so I called again, just trying to reach anybody . . . and back to general voice mail I went. Three or four days went by and again, no return phone call. I wondered, "What is going on?"

At this stage, I determined to hold up his document—his book, his words—in his company's face. I called and again went to general voice mail, but this time I left a long message. I stated the main purpose of my call and told them I also wanted to thank them for their book on organization and systems and how it had influenced my company and me. I also made it clear that, "I am disappointed that no one has gotten back to me. I think you should have someone checking voice mail and returning phone calls." I closed my message with, "I felt sure they would have had a simple system of returning phone calls in place!?"

Almost immediately, I got a phone call from one of the managers and an email from the author. I just used their own written document to remind them they should practice what they preach.

Words Have Meaning

Some have said that a mission statement is just another mania or business trend that consultants came up with, claiming it would turn companies around. Everybody in the business world began writing them. You may have written one yourself. But what happens to these statements is that people put them on a wall in a frame or they get lost in some drawer full of junk. Some business owners and managers never really take their mission statement seriously. I guess they figure if they write it and wait awhile, it will just happen—kind of like evolution.

Well, I can tell you, after ten years of deliberately trying to organize my company that order-from-chaos doesn't just happen. It takes a lot of creativity and hard work.

As you will see, I will use words, concepts or terms that some consultants and business gurus like to call "out-dated," saying, "People were doing that years ago, but now we've moved on to something new." That's because they are selling a slogan, a trend; something that appears "new" so you will buy the same thing over and over again. But nothing really changes. They know if you take a proven truth, stand on it, do it, and not give up until you have built an excellent company or organization, they can't repackage the truth for you with just trendy new words.

I was talking with a manager at a large company we were printing for and I used the word "problem." Can you believe the word "problem" was a problem?

He said, "Oh, we never use the word 'problem' here; we use the word 'opportunity' in its place. We tell our people, 'don't bring us a problem bring us an opportunity'.."

Okay, I get the message, and I get this new way of using the word, but please, I think the word "problem" explains a situation just fine. Yes, it's an old word, but I'm sure it will last another thousand years or so. This was a nice little catchy phrase a consultant taught this company, but their problem—oops! I mean opportunity—wasn't the particular words they were using. The problem was, they didn't *fix* the problems. By the way, they filed bankruptcy about a year later.

Downloading

All your company documents should be written and gathered together in your operations manual. This is the place to begin *downloading* your mind. Do you realize that you are storing in your brain's computer a very complex system of how your business operates? Some of you have been storing this information for years. The problem with carrying such information or systems around in your head is, people around you will keep logging into you like you are some kind of computer. They are just trying to get at the information you haven't bothered to download to a written document: a checklist, procedure or policy, etc.

That is why you are tired and stressed out!

Why You Can't Leave the Building Without Things Falling Apart!

You have become the mainframe computer that everyone in the organization is plugged into.

You can't blame your employees if they don't know exactly what you mean or exactly how to do a task the way you want it done, because you never bothered to write it down. You made it easy for them to use you as a computer, telephone book, operations manual, map, etc. Yes, you have become "Mama!" More about this later.

Imagine building a complex machine and you are the only one who really knows how it works. That is why an operations manual usually accompanies a product you buy. Think of your company as a machine . . . you will need an operations manual to show someone how it works.

I was talking with an engineer who owned his own business and he shared his idea that, "There are some things you just can't write down into a system."

I asked him to explain.

"Well," he said, "When I am ordering parts that we assemble into products for our business, I look at every invoice to see if we are getting good prices. When I order parts, I know how to negotiate for a better price."

I said, "You mean to tell me that you are a designer of electronic circuits and that you can't write a good system for purchasing?"

I recommended the following:

Make a list of the things you say while you're on the phone negotiating with these vendors for better prices. You could turn this into a checklist or procedure for your purchasing person or agent to use when buying. Maybe the lead statement, after the vendor has given your purchasing agent the price, is to tell them what price you paid last time, and that you were hoping for a better price this time. Or you could have your purchasing person call at least two or three vendors to get pricing. This would keep your main vendor accountable, while giving your purchasing person an edge in the negotiations. Yes, in some circumstance this may be a complex purchasing system, but you can write it down. It's in your head already; don't be lazy. Don't you realize, you only have to write it down once and then tweak it from time to time? Don't you realize you are freeing yourself from that particular job, each time you finish writing a system down, and that you can literally work your way out of all jobs in you organization, if you were so inclined. Don't leave a hole or a gap when you write out a system. You will have to try it out on someone to find the holes. You will also sleep better as you are clearing your mind of these systems.

Have you ever had a hard time sleeping, because you kept going over and over something in your head? So you finally get up and make a list or write the thing down. Your brain has to work constantly to keep all the systems of your organization or business fresh in your mind. It takes a lot of energy for your brain to maintain and update information.

I can't stress strongly enough the importance of downloading your business system or organization system into a written document—your operations manual. As you build this manual, it will become more and more valuable to you, to your employees, and to the worth of your business. You will gain freedom from jobs you should not have been burdened with in the first place.

You are the vision person; you should be spending your time looking down the road to see where your organization is going.

If you can't describe what you are doing as a process,
you don't know what you're doing.
W. Edward Deming

CHAPTER 4
WORKING ON YOUR BUSINESS, NOT IN IT

I HOPE BY now you can see that by working *on* your business, and not just *in* your business, you will gain the freedom to do the things you have always wanted to do, but couldn't find the time or the energy.

A lot of owners are doing the work of two or more people. They normally spend eight to twelve hours a day working in one or more of the positions in their organization.

So how will you ever find time to work on systems to really organize your business?

You may not like the answer, but this is what I did . . .

I worked at least two to four hours *extra* each day, and a lot of weekends, on the most important systems. I worked on designing system to fix the biggest leaks first. More about this later!

After about two years, things really started to roll and a former business owner who was counseling me at that time, made a good observation. He noticed I was spending most of my day taking in orders or acting as an inside customer service representative. He said, "Philip, I really think if you would train someone to take *your* place, you would have more time to work on your business."

So, I started to work on a system for customer service and order

entry—two of the positions I was working in myself. After I built
the system for these positions, I took the business owner's advice
and hired my daughter-in-law, Jennifer. I trained her on these systems for three months, eight hours a day, until she was doing about
80 percent of my job. Wow! I had six hours a day more to work on
the business! Things really started to move; and as she improved I
had even more time. Now I was at the top of the organization (See
chart page 25) and I couldn't believe the transformation that started
taking place.

You see, I didn't think I would ever be free of those positions,
even though I had already worked my way out of others, because
working in those positions gave me the controls I thought I needed
to make sure my business survived. I just couldn't see anyone else
doing them, until I understood the power of *systems*.

The solution will come as you install good systems. It will free
up more of your time. After you have built a complete system for the
position you are working in, then you need to hire someone, or delegate it to someone already on your staff. You need to train them on
the system for your position.

Once you work it so you really are only at the top of the organizational chart (see example on next page), and not trying to be all
things to all people, you will have the time to work on your vision
of becoming a great organization.

Your new position is to work *on* the business, not *in* it!

*All those things that most business owners long to do are not as
far off as you think!*

  •More time for family
      •Take a real vacation
          •Eliminate stress
              •Spend time on other projects
                  •Maybe start another enterprise
                      •Write a book?

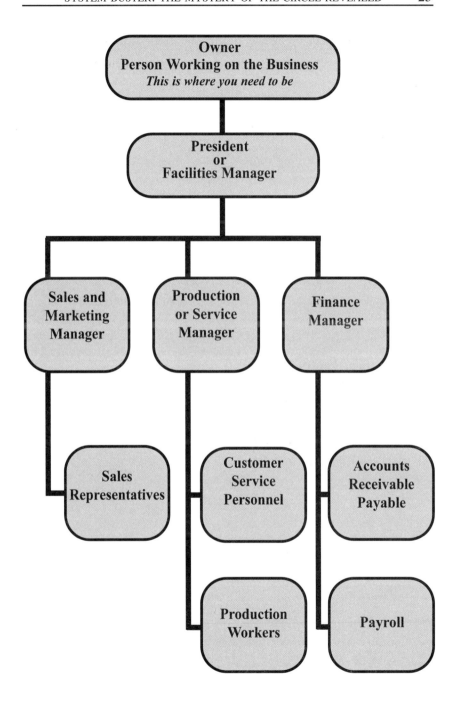

Working *on* your business—going the extra mile—will help you attain those goals and much more. You will own a business and not just have a job.

I spent my life stringing and unstringing my instrument, but the song I came to sing remains unsung.
Rabindranath Tagore-Waiting

Moreover you shall select from all the people able men, such as fear God, men of truth, hating covetousness; and place such over them to be rulers of thousands, rulers of hundreds, rulers of fifties, and rulers of tens.
And let them judge the people at all times. Then it will be that every great matter they shall bring to you, but every small matter they themselves shall judge. So it will be easier for you, for they will bear the burden with you.
If you do this thing, and God so commands you, then you will be able to endure, and all this people will also go to their place in peace.
Exodus 18:21-23

CHAPTER 5
WHAT ARE SYSTEMS?

Webster's Dictionary **Calls Systems:**

1. A group or arrangement of parts, facts, phenomena, etc, that relates to or interacts with each other in such a way as to form a whole;

2. An orderly method, plan or procedure

I call them *lifesavers*!

Think of a system as a circuit board that an engineer designs and tests until it works flawlessly. It should not have any breaks in the circuit, unless it is a planned break. Then the engineer puts this new circuit board, along with additional parts, into a nice clean package and the new electronic gadget works every time you turn it on. No need to go back to the schematic unless it needs repair. If you forget how a particular feature works, you just go to the *operations manual* for that gadget.

Imagine if, every time you turned on your new electronic gadget, it would stop working every few minutes and you would have to bang on it or take a wire and jump one of its circuits to get it working again. Well, that is what companies do when they design a poor system and don't spend the time to make it work flawlessly, and test how that system affects other systems in the company.

A Great System Supports a Company

I had a manager (I'll call her Helen) who was in charge of all the production departments. She was loved by the customers and had the respect of the employees, and everyone knew she "ruled the roost." For those who don't know what ruled the roost means, she was at the top of the pecking order. Well, that's enough about chickens. I mean she was the top dog, the kingpin, bad to the bone. You get the picture! But Helen was beginning to have some personal issues and came to me with her resignation. I did not want her to leave; however, I understood her situation. Other managers and other people in our company started coming to me to ask, "What are we were going to do without Helen?" I told them that Helen, although a fine person, was not the main reason things ran so well in production. It was the systems we had been building, for nine years at that time that was the reason production ran so well. Helen's title was production manager, but that really meant that she managed the *production manager system*. Do you understand what I just said? Helen managed our company's production manager *system*. It wasn't the Helen management system.

We had built a system for our company that was very detailed and complete. We completed the circuit and removed the gaps in the production management wheel to keep it rolling along smoothly. The person that replaced Helen was trained quickly on the production management system. In fact, it is running better now, and with less effort, because we keep improving the system.

Please understand what I am saying here. Good systems don't replace people, but they eliminate the need for excessive personnel. Payroll is your number one expense. It's because people *are* important that you need a great system to support and develop great employees. Overstaffing sends many companies into bankruptcy. Systems tell you how much personnel you need.

If you measure an employee's ability on a scale of one-to-ten, if someone is a five then with a great system they could be as effective as an eight or a nine. Just imagine if the employee was an eight or a nine. We now have such employees. As the system improves and transforms the organization, the people that the organization attracts will improve. This production manager change was more confirmation to our employees as to the importance of the system.

The Mystery of the Circles

One night when I was about 28 years old and sitting on my front porch in Louisiana, I had what I thought was a real vision—but I always had an active imagination. I was looking up at the stars, and suddenly I could see circles of all sizes. It came to me that everything in the universe was represented by these circles, and these circles represented systems. All of the circles intersected and seemed to interact with each other. And I realized that every circle or every system in the universe affects every other circle or system in the universe. That's it! That was my vision. The very night that happened, I began to ponder this mystery of the circles:

A group of people is like a circle of friends that affects every member in their group and their group affects and interacts with other "circles" of people. Everyone on this planet is affected in some way by every other person on the planet. The planets, solar systems, stars and galaxies are all systems of circles, and every planet affects the other planets, as one galaxy affects another galaxy, and so on, and so on into infinity.

Well, back to earth! The *circle* in the title of this book represents a completed system with no gaps, like the closed-circuit system I will reveal later.

It is He that sits above the circle of the earth, and the inhabitants are like grasshoppers; Who stretches out the heavens like a curtain, and spreads them out like a tent to dwell in.
Isaiah 40:22

CHAPTER 6
WHAT REPLACES SYSTEMS IN MOST ORGANIZATIONS?

Managers, Managers, Managers

Ever wonder why many companies are top-heavy with managers and assistant managers? It's because they don't have good systems, so they hire managers to manage the chaos.

Imagine a system as a wheel with gaps in it. Every time the wheel rolls to the spot where the gap is, it stops. Now imagine this gap is a hole in a company's system. Instead of building a system without gaps, companies hire managers to push the wheel of production and service to get it rolling again when it gets bogged down or stops in the gaps. Then another manager will push it again until it stops at the next gap, and so on. Then they will hire an assistant manager to help the manager when the gap is too big for one person to keep it rolling. So, instead of putting in place a good system, or even having a system, they insert more and more managers into the gaps. Managers should only be hired to manage and improve the system, not to be running to and fro managing chaos and putting out fires. I call our system "*System100*" because it is a complete circuit, a *complete circle* and a comprehensive system that is 100 percent and nothing less.

<u>COMPLETE</u>

Having all needed or normal parts, elements or details; lacking
nothing. Entire, thoroughly wrought, finished. Perfect.

There is no such thing as 110 percent complete, just like a circuit
on a circuit board, it is either complete (100 percent) or its not. If it's
less than 100 percent it will not work properly and if it's complete it
will run and run.

Another manager I hired had come from a company that was
three or four times larger that our company. He had managed fifty
or more employees and had experienced "burn-out" at his former
company because just to keep up, he consistently worked sixty to
seventy hours a week. He wanted to move to the south, so he
answered an ad we had placed for a pre-press manager. Let's call
him Sam. I thought Sam was the answer to helping us meet the goals
we had set for the pre-press department. Even before his arrival, we
had the pre-press department very clean and systemized. We trained
him on our system and I thought certainly with his background, running our well-organized pre-press would be a cinch. But after he was
with us for two or three weeks, the department started to deteriorate
and our customer service people were getting concerned.

I called him into a meeting and he seemed to be very cooperative. I said, "Sam, these are the concerns I have . . ." and he wrote
them down and said he would handle them immediately. Nothing
changed. In fact, it was getting worse by the day, so I called him to
my office again. This time he started complaining about "too many
hours." I went over our concerns again and he said he would take
care of them. A week or so later, he was called out of town on an
emergency and I told our production manager that I wanted to run
the pre-press until he returned. It would give me the opportunity to
see how far the systems had actually broken down and to find out
why Sam was struggling. I found Sam's desk and other pre-press
cabinets to be a wreck. Notes that he had taken in our meetings and
other important papers were just buried in piles of paper in the

bottom of drawers. He was the type of manager that just hid things, instead of dealing with issues. I found he had lost a lot of our templates and had disregarded other systems we used as major time savers. None of them were being utilized. He was *off* the system and that was the reason for the problems we were having.

When he got back to the office, I met with him again. I said, "Sam, I see why you are working the long hours you have been complaining about. You have departed from our system and now you are way off course." I told him while he was gone and I was working in his place, I had started a job and found the pre-press templates missing, so I had to start the job from scratch. It took me three extra hours to complete it and I believed he had been doing it from scratch every time. I said, "Do you know how many hours you lose a week from not using just the template system?" He said he lost the templates. I asked him why he had not rebuilt them. He had no answer, just a blank stare.

I told Sam that while he was gone I had estimated he was losing ten to fifteen hours a week of time by not using our systems. That was where all the long hours he said he had been working are going. When we fail to file things and bury them in some drawer or cabinet it causes turmoil later and costs even more time.

I said, "Sam, I am totally confused! How did you run the whole production of a company four times the size of ours?"

He said, "Oh, I had several assistant managers and they did a lot of the work."

I asked him, "Sam, don't you realize that if you would stick to the system you wouldn't have to work sixty or seventy hours a week?" I know he wouldn't have needed all those assistant managers at his old company with an excellent system.

Yes, I had to give him his leave, but I still considered it a constructive thing for me to have gone through that with Sam. It clearly demonstrates how systems make money by saving time. How you maintain your work area speaks volumes. Sometimes people look you in the eye, as Sam did, and say, "Yes . . . oh sure, I'll take care of that," but their actions say "No!" They are betting no one will follow up on them, so they'll just ignore it.

I went by the field of the lazy man,
and by the vineyard of the man devoid of understanding;
And there it was, all overgrown with thorns;
its surface was covered with weeds;
Its stone wall was broken down. When I saw it,
I considered it well; I looked on it
and received instruction: A little sleep, a little slumber,
a little folding of the hands to rest:
So shall your poverty come like a prowler
and your need like an armed man.
Proverbs 24:30-34

Meetings, Meetings, Meetings

"Why do some companies have so many meetings?" you ask. Most of the time, it is because they don't have good systems. Every organization has problems and this is the conventional way that businesses deal with them. Meetings are called to get everybody "on the same page" or to tell people to *remember* to do something.

A meeting may go like this:

Sally forgot something that a customer had requested and blames Joe. Joe blames Bob and Bob blame Sue, but they seem to get it all worked out in this lengthy meeting, which just cost the company a lot of money. *The cost:* Everyone in the meeting, times their salary, for time spent in the meeting. And the next week, it starts all over again. Someone calls another meeting because there are more problems to deal with, and some of the old ones are back again.

Do you realize it can cost companies hundreds to thousands of dollars for a single meeting? Next time you are in a meeting, run some numbers to see how much that meeting cost. If the issues that needed to be solved in meetings were placed in a system—a daily routine checklist, written procedure or policy or some other written system—most meetings would not be needed at all.

Meeting time should be spent brain-storming or doing other visionary work, not used in place of a poor system or a manager or owner that is too lazy to fix problems with a proper system.

When you tell people to just remember to do this or that, you are gambling with the results. In most companies, people are already expected to remember too much. I have had employees say to me, "You know, you rarely have meetings with us." I tell them it is because we have systems to fix problems and a meeting of that type is not needed here. We do have scheduled meetings to fix systems and for other creative work. Those are really productive because they fix the problem and ideas are born. How much money do you think you would save with fewer meetings? We have saved a lot.

For a dream cometh through the multitude of business,
and a fool's voice through a multitude of words.
Ecclesiastes 5:3

CHAPTER 7
ENCOUNTERING OPPOSITION

WHEN YOU START building and putting in systems, you can plan on opposition! This is where leadership comes into play. *Systems work! It's not a theory, but a fact!* If you want to improve your organization, then be ready to take a stand. And also be ready to be humbled!

One day in the early years of building our systems, my son Paul came into my office and said, "Dad, why do you take so much grief from Bob, our graphics manager? Bob enjoys doing everything he can to find fault and problems with the systems you are trying to build. He is mocking you and laughing behind your back and saying these systems will never work."

I said, "Paul, its okay . . . I am *using* Bob!"

Paul asked, "What do you mean?"

I said, "Although Bob is a pain in my side and I would love sometimes to show him the door, he does find the holes and gaps in the system. Paul, imagine a system where Bob couldn't find any holes. What would we have?"

Paul replied, "A great system!"

I said, "*That* is what we are trying to build . . . and we will build it!"

I'm no psychiatrist, but there are people in this world who like a little chaos; some are attracted to a lot of chaos. I've met them, observed them and, yes, even confronted them. My conclusion is that they feel safe somehow, because they can hide in the confusion. They can point fingers and blame others because in a chaotic organization with no systems, who could prove otherwise? When a manager or an owner's attention is diverted away because of chaos and lack of systems, a lot of hiding the truth and monkey business goes on.

Have you ever seen the gorillas on TV's Animal Planet running around kicking up dust and shaking the branches? It's quite a show, and it looks as if a lot of activity is going on there. All the other gorillas are very impressed with the commotion. But it's all smoke and mirrors—just a big ole show for the folks. In a company that is chaotic, people can do the same thing; looking busy, running to and fro, but they are just kicking up dust. Some managers may be impressed with the bustle of an employee and when they pass them they will hear things like, "Whew, rough day, I'm worn out!" Or those famous words, "We need more help!" These kinds of folks do not care for a structured system because they will be exposed by it and you will encounter their opposition.

Other people feel insecure about their abilities, and the system is asking them questions they have never had to answer. Their pride, talent and organizational abilities are being challenged.

Some of these people have come from companies, where they were believed to be talented, organized and very knowledgeable. Because their old company had no systems, this person was celebrated because they looked very impressive. You see some people may see themselves as a nine on a scale of one-to-ten, but when they encounter a well-structured system, they may be exposed as a five. This type of person doesn't like a system and, again . . . opposition.

I am telling you these stories because you must decide if you are ready for the challenge. Will you stand?

For which of you, intending to build a tower, does not sit down first and count the cost, whether he has enough to finish it .
Luke 14:28

No 'Sacred Cows'

I had a very skilled department manager in my company. I thought, at that time, that I couldn't do without "John." He was highly technical, and a very dependable employee. John had been with us in relocating our company from one part of town to another. However, the system was showing that he had some work habits that needed improving. I had a meeting with John and told him the things that needed improvement. He said he would work on the bad work habits, but after a few months the system was telling me that it still wasn't fixed and that John was still not adhering to the system. I had to make a very difficult decision at that time. Do I tell others in our company they have to adhere to the system, but because I may be thinking of John as some kind of "sacred cow"—an essential employee that I'm afraid to lose—I will continue to make an exception for John's behavior? If I did that, I may as well stop right now and throw the years of building systems that were transforming us into a great company right out the window.

By that time, I had invested eight years into building our systems and I couldn't look my son in the eyes anymore and tell him we can't do without John. The rubber was about to meet the road. *The systems were either what I claimed them to be, or they weren't.* I met with John and again told him that he was either going to have to adhere to the system or he would have to leave.

He said, "Well, to tell you the truth, I really don't like systems."

I said, "John, thank you for telling me the truth. I know you don't, but I am sold on them because I have seen the benefit for our customers, employees and myself by having them."

We parted friends and our company saw an immediate improvement in production and other systems. We didn't miss a step. As a manager, John was hindering our progress. This decision sent a message to all of our employees, that I would not yield to anyone's not adhering to the system, and that we would stay the course on continual improvement.

I had a lady sit down in my office after only a few weeks working at our company and tell me that it was hard to work at our company. She said she was not used to being called out on every mistake. I told her that I, nor her supervisor, were bringing up the mistakes—the system was pointing them out. I told her she should be glad that the mistakes were found, because when she makes them, the system also demands that we show her how to correct it. Today she is learning her job and the company is benefiting.

Yes, there will be opposition, but if our goal is a successful business, we must take a stand!

Cast out the scoffer and contention will leave, yes, strife and reproach will cease.
Proverbs 22:10

CHAPTER 8
ARE YOU ON THE RUN?

I LEARNED A lot about chickens when I was a boy. After my mother died suddenly, I went to live with my Aunt Ducy in Pearl River, Louisiana. I was nine years old, and the fact that my aunt raised chickens, along with other small farm animals, helped to keep my mind off more serious things then. Chickens can be very funny. But when Aunt Ducy's chickens got to a certain age, we needed to get them ready for market. *My* job was to catch the chicken (*that* was funny), and hand it to Aunt Ducy. Then I'd stand off about ten feet while she would very calmly lay the chicken's head on the stump, raise her little hatchet . . . and whack! *Not* so funny—but so goes farm life! I learned that when a chicken loses its head, it will often run around in circles for a time, until it runs out of steam and keels over. Reminds me of some businesses I've observed! A company without a good "head" for systems is apt to flail around for a while, but it will eventually collapse. In the same way, if a leader fails to download the systems he keeps in his head, then eventually—if he should leave the business for any reason—the systems go with him, and the business is in danger of collapsing. This is why a lot of *second-generation* businesses fail.

Earlier, we talked about how you need to download so all that information you carry around in your head is readily available to your staff (and so they won't feel the need to corner you every time you do a walk-through of your company or department). Have you grown tired of having one staff member after another pull you aside to ask you the same questions for the umpteenth time?

Have you given your staff a manual where they can find the answers for themselves? No? Okay, so they will continue to pull at you like a small child tugging on its mother's skirt while she has both hands in the sink, the phone's ringing, and another child is crying for attention.

"Hey Bob! You think you could get me a . . ."
"Hey Bob! My uncle is visiting. I would like a little time . . ."
"Hey Bob! Can you have this light fixed . . ."
"Hey Bob! Would you talk to so and so about . . ."

This gets old! The reason owners and managers get burned out is because they have no systems to handle all these questions and pressures. It's not very hard then to understand why some of them hide out, sneak in and out of the building, close their doors to employees and problems. No surprise that they have glassy, far away looks in their eyes; throw tantrums and attend "Happy Hour" frequently!

In his E-Myth book, Mr. Gerber wrote:

YOU are the problem
YOU have always been the problem
YOU will always be the problem
. . . until YOU change

I can tell you, I thought long and *hard* about that!

Denial ain't just a river in Egypt.
Mark Twain

Charles Edward Deming of the famed Deming Award for Manufacturing says, "You should not expect your employees to do the job the way you think they should, unless you have provided them the necessary tools and the time in which to complete it."

In other words, if your employees come running up to you every time you walk through the various departments to ask you every question under the sun, then you haven't given them the tools or the systems to do their job.

It's Your Own Fault—YOU Are the Problem!

One of the demonstrations Dr. Deming would do at his seminars with managers and CEOs of some very large corporations, involved bringing a group of them to the front of the room and giving each one a box of black and white marbles all mixed together. He would tell them that their assignment was to separate the white marbles from the black marbles and he would give them one minute in which to do it. He assured them it could be done in one minute or less, because he had done it himself. He would then start the timer and the managers and CEOs would start separating the marbles into different boxes just as fast as they could, while everyone was laughing and cheering them on. After one minute, he would say stop! Everyone would look around to see if anybody had completed the separation, and of course no one had. Then he would ask them, "Why didn't you complete the job? You expect your employees to do jobs in a certain amount of time and when they don't, you get upset." He continued, "In a lot of cases, you have never tested the job to see how long it takes—to see if it can be consistently done in a certain amount of time. You don't supply them with the correct tools or systems to do the job in the allotted time.

"I gave *you* a job and you couldn't do it in the time I said it could be done. The reason why you couldn't do it is that I didn't give you the tool to do it."

At that point, Dr. Deming would pull another box with holes drilled in it from under a table. He would start the clock, pour the box of mixed black and white marbles into the box with the holes, then he would shake it around, and only the black marbles would fall through. Because the white marbles were too large to fall through the holes, they would remain in the box. Deming completed the job of separating the marbles in about thirty seconds.

What is the moral to this story? Okay kids, all together . . .

GIVE YOUR EMPLOYEES THE RIGHT TOOLS AND SYS-TEMS AND THEY WILL CONSISTENTLY COMPLETE THE TASK TO YOUR SPECIFICATIONS . . . AND ON TIME.

Give instruction to a wise man and he will be wiser still.
Proverbs 9:9

CHAPTER 9
GUILTY AS CHARGED,
BUT DON'T GO BACK

. . . BACK TO HIDING from the truth, back to sweeping things under the rug, back to not fixing the problems . . . back to "The Land of Chaos."

According to scripture, after Israel endured 400 years of slavery in Egypt, Moses (with no small help from God) was able to set his people free. But after coming into some hardships and inconvenience, the Israelites began to grumble. They told Moses how good they'd had it in Egypt. Amazing! In a very short time, they had forgotten the cruel beatings, working in the mud pits, the back breaking labor, moving tons of stone to build Pharoah's tomb—and all this with no compensation. You see, the Israelites had grown accustomed to the chaos and humiliating situation, even though God had assured them they were the people of promise. They even threatened to stone Moses for leading them out of bondage. But Moses persevered; and year-after-year he led the people toward the Promised Land. He faced the opposition and refused to turn back, because his eyes were set on the vision—the bigger picture. He knew where he was going and how great it would be for everyone when they finally got there. Moses was a true leader.

Yes, it can be really discouraging in the face of opposition. But this thing only works if you expect nothing but the *truth*! If you will lead, you will find those people who will follow you on your mission to becoming a world-class organization.

Good systems tend to expose lazy or incompetent employees, but they also expose the *good* ones. And isn't that what you want? I have found that good employees love a good system—while the others will often see your systematic way of organizing as "too rigid."

People who balk at systems will tell you they prefer a "relaxed, family-type" atmosphere. Well, I call it a "loosy-goosey, shoot-from-the-hip, let-the-good-times-roll, as-long-as-it's-not-my-money-and-I'm-getting-paid-I'm-happy" atmosphere. Here is what they are really saying: "I want an atmosphere that doesn't require stewardship or accountability. I want an atmosphere where I can make all the personal phone calls I want . . . visit or gossip with everyone in the building when I want . . . play on the Internet when I want . . . take as many smoke breaks as I want . . . take my cat to the vet when I want . . . work the hours I want . . . and complain about everything under the sun, including the boss, when I want." These will also complain at holiday time when they don't get the bonus they want. Go figure!

If you, as an employer, won't stand up to this type of opposition and intimidation, then I can tell you right now, you are wasting your time in reading this book. You don't have what it takes! The only thing you *may* have left . . . is a prayer!

Building a great organization—notice *organization* is the key word here—takes commitment! It takes leadership and your willingness to lead when people are murmuring and wanting you to return to Egypt—the "Land of Chaos."

But, if you will turn your face into the winds of opposition, stay the course, and journey on, you will reach the land of peace and prosperity—*joy* even! The rewards will be priceless.

If you faint in the day of adversity, your strength is small.
Proverbs 24:10

CHAPTER 10
LEADERSHIP:
THE BUCK STOPS HERE

Leadership

Dr. John C. Maxwell, founder of The Injoy Group, has written several very interesting books on leadership. Recently, a friend gave me his devotional book, *The 21 Most Powerful Minutes in a Leader's Day* in which he writes, "To go to the highest level you have to develop leaders; then you should develop leaders of leaders. Many leaders want to make followers, but at that rate you will only add to your organization one person at a time. But leaders who develop leaders multiply their growth, because for every leader they develop, they also receive all of that leader's followers."

Dr. Maxwell's book also says to, "Hire the best staff you can find, develop them as much as you can, and hand off everything you possibly can to them."

I agree with this premise for the most part. However, I am firmly convinced that, to pass your vision on to someone affectively, it must be in *written* form. Also, a good system assures the leader you are developing that he or she will have a greater chance at success. *Your system is a powerful tool to give to this leader.* As I mentioned earlier, the power of a system is that you don't have to start over every time you replace one leader with another.

Yes, I suppose you could hire a leader to set up the whole system, and you could go on your merry way, but I believe that's when it turns into *their* vision and not yours. Later, if that leader decides to leave, you wouldn't know where they began or where they left off. You would have to find another leader, throw them into the last leader's position, and tell them to "Swim!" They would ask, "How and where?" And you would say, "You are a leader—figure it out!"

I always look for people who are smarter and more talented than I am. Over the past couple of years, when I interview people, I tell every one of them I am looking for a *leader*, not just an employee to fill a position.

Okay, let's go back to my band days, when I was a lead singer and hired my own band. I always hired musicians who could *also* sing. I wanted the best singers I could find. I had everyone in my band singing lead at some point in our show. I often had people tell me, "Philip, your bass player" . . . or other musician . . . "sings better than you!" I wasn't intimidated by better singers; I learned from them, and it only made the *Philip Paul and Patrol Show* all the better. I had people who thought I was "great" and some who thought I stunk. But, so what! Not everyone was going to like me. There is probably no singer on the planet that ever took to the stage where everyone was a fan. To sell a million CDs in the U.S. you only need one out of every 350 people to like you and buy your CD.

To become great, you are wise to surround yourself with great people!

Iron sharpens iron, So one man sharpens another.
Proverbs 27:17

I not only use all the brains I have, but all I can borrow.
Woodrow Wilson

President Harry S. Truman kept a sign on his desk in the White House that read, THE BUCK STOPS HERE. In his farewell address to the American people, given in January 1953, President Truman referred to this sign by saying, "The President — whoever he is — has to decide. He can't pass the buck to anybody. No one else can do the deciding for him. That's his job!"

You must be willing to accept the truth about a situation and deal with it. You are responsible for *all* the decisions made in your company — even the ones made by your managers and employees.

As I mentioned earlier, we have developed a software program called *System100*. The program has a button on it that says, THE BUCK STOPS HERE. All employees at our company have access to the program and can click on that button. In the comments field, they can type in any serious problem(s) they are having and it is emailed directly to my home. This is not a system for suggestions of continual improvement.

This particular system serves a very important function and has only been used a few times. It is to be used when a manager or another person in the company is mistreating someone or is doing something that is dishonest, and they are afraid of retaliation from the other person. When someone uses this system, I will very discreetly call them in for a meeting and assure them that the information they sent me is between me and them. If they will not allow me to use this information to improve the situation, then I tell them it's useless information. However, I believe communication is key in all good systems and, if an employee *does* want to resolve the issue, all parties should then be brought together and this information put out on the table for each to give their side of the story.

I have found that when you bring people together to discuss serious accusations or problems — stories tend to be revised. I want my employees to know that they can tell me the truth, and feel safe telling their manager or supervisor the truth, without being mistreated or alienated for speaking out.

The only way you can truly fix a problem or make good decisions is to determine the real truth of the matter. The Buck Stops

Here system is not to be used to spy on anyone or to play one person against the other. But as the leader, you need to know that you are ultimately responsible for the well being of your employees while they are at work. If a manager or supervisor is intimidating your employees not to speak the truth or not to tell you what is really going on, then you can only go so far with improving the organization and reaching the goals of your mission.

The Buck Stops Here system also sends a strong message to your managers and supervisors that they are not better than others in the organization, they just have a different position and they will also be held accountable for their decision not to improve the system by ignoring or squashing the truth. Sometimes managers don't want to hear the truth because, when they know the truth, they also know they have to deal with it and, quite frankly, some just don't want to deal with real issues.

Remember, their decisions are your decisions, and as I said before, The Buck Stops Here system has rarely been used, because it really serves as a *deterrent* to that kind of problem.

It is not good to show partiality in judgment.
Proverbs 24:23

CHAPTER 11
SYSTEM ORGANIZATIONS, TYPES AND PEOPLE

TQM

Total Quality Management is a system of continual improvement in every phase of a business. It is a process by which every person in a business, from the highest in management to the grounds keeper, is part of *learning* the system, *operating and using* the system and *improving* the system.

In the chapter titled, "Are You on the Run?" I mentioned Edward Deming, the namesake of the Deming Award for Manufacturing. He was another source from which I learned about the importance of good systems, and how they work.

Edward Deming was an American whose ideas of continual improvement and total quality management were rejected by American auto (and other) manufacturers until about 1980. At one time America controlled most of world's automobile manufacturing market and didn't see the need for improvement. At the end of World War II, Edward Deming went to Japan to conduct a census for the U. S. Government as part of the rebuilding of Japan. While in Japan, the Union of Japanese Scientist and Engineers had heard of Deming's quality theories and invited him to give a lecture. The Japanese were so inspired by his theories of quality and continual improvement that some of the largest manufacturers, such as Toyota and other companies, implemented his ideas into their manufacturing. As you may know, Japanese business was starting from the ground up after the devastation of World War II. In the 1950s, a product with the mark "Made in Japan" was thought of as junk. I remember, as a kid, hearing people laugh about and mocking Japanese products. But getting on into the 1960s and 1970s, we all stopped laughing.

In fact, American businesses became very fearful of Japanese products, because the little Toyota, bought as a "second car," was lasting ten years with hardly any maintenance, and the big American family car was falling apart and constantly in need of repairs. Well, you know what happened next. Americans bought more and more Japanese cars and Japan started to take a large share of the market. Through the continual improvement system, Japanese cars got better and better. Every part of their car was gone over to see how they could improve it, continually.

Today, The Edward Deming Award is the highest award you can receive in Japan for manufacturing. After we had lost a lot of the world market and Edward Deming was in his 80s, we finally woke up.

A story goes that the president of Ford Motors invited Dr. Deming to give Ford management a seminar on his total quality and continual improvement system. Just after he introduced Dr. Deming on the day of the seminar, the president of Ford started to leave the room. At that, Dr. Deming walked off the podium and caught up with the president and said, "If you're leaving, so am I," and started to walk out. Well, they got Deming to come back, and so did the president of Ford. Deming was sending a message to the president that "you have to know the system."

Ford implemented Deming's systems, and so did General Motors and other manufacturers. Why? Fear. They were losing business fast. But the arrogance continued for a while.

They told Dr. Deming, "We want you to implement your systems in our company, and we would like you to start working with mid-management and on down to production."

Dr. Deming said, "No! You don't seem to understand. The system starts with *you*. It starts at the *top*—because if upper management doesn't understand the system and are not committed to the system, then they will make decisions that will hinder or wreck the system. The system starts with you, Mr. CEO/President! *You* must be trained first!"

Again, it was fear that motivated Ford and General Motors to give Americans the quality they deserved, and only because they were losing business to the Japanese. I know I don't want to lose business due to poor quality, service or lack of continually improving! We ought to thank the Japanese for their dedication to quality; otherwise, we still might be driving piles of junk. I have owned three Ford vans since the "Quality is Job 1" marketing campaign started. Every one of them have been great. In fact, my first Ford van was used for a delivery van and my personal transportation. We put 250,000 miles on it and then gave it to my son who drove it another 50,000 miles, then sold it.

Thanks, Japan, for kicking us in the rear end! We have been the benefactor!

ISO Standards

You may or may not be familiar with ISO, the International Standards Organization that is headquartered in Geneva, Switzerland. Maybe you've seen their large banners, on the sides of buildings that say CERTIFIED ISO 9000, and didn't know what it was!? The 9000, is just a type of certification.

ISO is an organization that sets high standards for quality control and other management control systems. It was set up to help companies standardize quality control systems, services and other business practices. The standard set up by ISO is used by companies all over the world. One really effective policy used by the Japanese in making great cars, is to buy parts and services only from companies that have strict quality controls, continual improvement systems, and who share the same goals and ideas for quality and service. Let's say, for example, if a company makes headlights, the

Japanese manufacturer not only insists on a quality headlight, but also a promise from the vendor that the headlight will be continually improved. And the vendor has to prove that they will be continually improving that headlight.

Now imagine, each part of their cars getting better each and every year. Every time a Japanese car or part comes back as defective, they gather all the people responsible for those defects and come up with ideas to improve the system so it won't happen again. They don't come together just to place blame. No, they want to *fix* the problem as a team. They are not interested in trying to cover up problems; they are interested in gaining market share by making a great car.

We had an inspector from Nintendo come to audit our systems. They wanted to be assured we had, and could prove we had, quality printing and service, because our printing would reflect on their product and they demand quality. Since we have most of the control systems required by ISO, and since we've been operating these quality systems and services, we were able to be certified to print Nintendo products. They want their products printed by a company that shares their values and quality standards. Nintendo is ISO-certified. We have had several ISO-certified companies visit our facility for inspections. *We understand that through good systems we can compete at the highest levels.* Today, business is becoming a global market and we must keep improving in order to compete on the world stage, as well as the local market.

No need to be anxious about ISO. Let me tell you a little story.

When I started on my mission, I read an article about ISO and became very curious. I called a firm that consults with companies to set up ISO standards to get them certified. I didn't even know what ISO was. The article about ISO and the system of continual improvement sounded like something I ought to look into. Well, I got someone on the phone at this firm and started asking him questions about ISO. I didn't understand a thing he was saying, but—so as not to sound totally ignorant—I asked him to send me the manual and other literature about ISO.

He asked me, "How many employees do you have?"

I said, "Five, including myself." (This was ten years ago.)

There was a long pause on the other end of the phone and then he said, "No, you don't understand, Mr. Beyer, this is for large companies! The cost is upwards of a quarter of a million dollars to implement. You will need to hire a consultant to help you implement and understand these systems. They have people to write policies and procedures for you."

Not wanting to be talked out of it, I told him I planned on being a large company one day and I needed to get started right away, understanding ISO systems. He sent me the manual. Well, he was right! When I received the manual and literature, I opened them and started reading. It didn't make much sense, at that point. Terms like "Non-Conforming Processes" and others they used were hard for me to understand. I picked up a word or two and a couple of ideas, but not very much.

I continued to build my systems on my own. When you are managing a business, you know what needs to be fixed and you don't need ISO or anyone else to tell you that, because it's already happening to you. After a few years of building systems, I picked up the ISO manual again and I was amazed that I understood a lot more of it. After a few more years, I opened it again and I had more understanding. I realized that I was doing the same things I just had different names for my systems. Eventually, the entire ISO manual made sense.

You remember earlier I was talking about Nintendo being ISO-Certified, and the inspector auditing our systems. Well, as he was leaving he turned to me and said, "You have one of the most organized and cleanest printing plants I have ever audited. In fact, I believe you could pass and be ISO-certified, if you wanted to." I was on cloud nine. It was one of those proud moments at Beyer Printing.

A friend told me that the president of a very large commercial printing company in California, where she sold printing, had told her that ISO was just a gimmick and used as a marketing tool. This president also said he didn't need systems; he just needed good people.

My friend told me that two out of three jobs she shipped to her customers had something wrong with them. But when she would complain, the production manager would throw a tantrum and try to intimidate her. One day she reported his behavior to this president and he told her the reason that she was hired was to smooth things over with the customers—that these production problems were just part of the printing business. What he was really saying was that she was hired to make excuses (lie) for the company because they were too lazy and arrogant to fix their problems by incorporating good systems. This type of person would have you believe ISO or any proven system was a gimmick. Apparently, they believe it is easier to tear something down, make excuses, and go golfing, than to build a system that eliminates internal chaos. It's not about their customers and employees—it's about them! Let me assure you, the ISO system and our system are not fads, nor gimmicks. They work! But you must use it correctly.

Which "Type" Are You?

Michael Gerber's book *The E-Myth* talks about three types of people in an organization—entrepreneurs, managers and technicians. It's important to identify people's skills and interests within an organization to make sure you have the right people in the right positions.

The ENTREPRENEUR envisions or starts an enterprise. They are self-starters. But they sometimes lack organizational skills, and they are not always known for being good business people because of it. You see them going from one project to the next and sometimes never completing any of them. They can become bored quickly doing one thing, because their mind is usually off thinking about another thing—a new invention, idea or project. Entrepreneurs see opportunity around every corner and sometimes lack the discipline *not* to chase every rabbit they see. If you are an entrepreneur, then organization may elude you because you have too many irons in the fire or too many ideas going on at one time. So you need managers and technicians to put feet to your ideas.

Think of your business like the new invention of a gadget. Take your creative talent and focus it on building your business. Reinvent your business into the world's best-run gadget. After you turnkey your business, you may want to sell it and then move on to the next "gadget."

The MANAGER tends to have good leadership and organizational skills that help to build the business. Their work is to manage and improve the system, and sometimes to create systems. A manager should be trained not to manage people, but to manage the system.

The TECHNICIAN has the skills to do the hands-on work of the organization—or you could say they shape the stones and move them into place. The technician's work is to implement the system and play a vital role in improving the system.

PLEASE NOTE: A system doesn't know an entrepreneur, from a manager, from a technician, from a cow in the road. The system will only work as long as everyone uses it correctly.

And a good system knows when you are NOT!

But now God has set the members, each one of them,
in the body just as He pleased. And if they were all one member,
where would the body be? But now indeed there are many
members, yet only one body. So the eye cannot say to
the hand, "I have no need of you"; Nor again the head
cannot say to the feet, "I have no need of you."
I Corinthians 12:18-21

CHAPTER 12
WHY BE COMMITTED
TO A SYSTEM?

WITH A GOOD system, people in your organization have a clear understanding of the work they are to perform and what is expected of them. Without a system there are many unanswered questions and quality and service cannot be guaranteed.

Most companies don't have systems with written standards that give people the proper tools by which to accomplish their job. In these types of companies, when a new manager comes in, the whole system may change. You may have been in a situation where, if there's a qualified manager, operations run better. If an unqualified manager comes along later, operations start falling apart. With a great system, operations remain stable; expectations and standards remain the same, no matter *who* the manager is. The System should set the agenda.

Do you think McDonald's, the hamburger giant, changes their whole way of managing, or changes their system, when they change managers, personnel or even franchise owners? NO WAY! The new managers and personnel *learn* the McDonald's system. They *follow* the system, and in turn are followed up with by the managers of the system to make sure they are adhering to that system. However, McDonald's franchise owners and all levels of personnel are encouraged to help *improve* the system. But they learn the present system first.

My son, Paul, and I decided to grab a cup of coffee at a McDonald's right up the street from our business, and while standing in line, I noticed empty coffee creamers piling up by the coffee pot. I said, "Hey, Paul, look . . . a breakdown in the McDonald's System! They should put a container there with a small sign or label that says 'place your empty coffee creamers here.'"

A few days later, we had to laugh when we were back getting a cup of coffee. There it was. Without my saying a word, someone had added a container and a sign that said, PLACE YOUR EMPTY COFFEE CREAMERS HERE. It was a great little demonstration to my son Paul and me of how the system of continual improvement works.

But let's break it down a little further.

THE COMPANY as a Reason to be Committed to a System

What is the main reason a business is in business? It's to make a profit! In some corners of today's society, profit has become a dirty word. However, profit has to be the main goal in order for the company to exist—but not the only goal. With a successful company that makes profits, you can afford to give back to your community in countless ways. If it weren't for many great American companies, we wouldn't have some of the schools, libraries, hospitals, research centers and many other blessings that their *profits* have provided; not to mention the jobs they create. They have also been used in time of war to maintain our freedoms. Therefore, to help assure prosperity—which I believe is profit with peace and joy attached—you will need a great system.

THE CUSTOMER as a Reason to be Committed to a System

If you promise great quality and service to customers, then you need a system to back it up. Therefore, you're able to *prove your promise* and it's not just a slogan on your business card. A system is the only proven way to obtain consistent results.

The system helps the sales and marketing department bring in more customers. Remember I told you about Nintendo's quality manager saying we had one of the cleanest and most organized printing companies he had ever inspected? Our sales department prospected and delivered the Nintendo customer to our door, but it was *the system* that closed the deal.

A company should grow regardless of whether you add sales people or not. If you are delivering good quality and good service at a fair price, you will grow. *The system* will help you in guaranteeing that quality and service.

THE EMPLOYEE as a Reason to be Committed to a System

A system lets management know which employees are performing well and which are not.

Performance should not be based on a feeling you get of how someone is performing, it should be based on facts that come from having a system that measures performance.

Have you ever been in a situation where you were working very hard and the person next to you was a slacker? But the supervisor never seemed to notice this person's laziness, because when the supervisor would come around, this person would kick up a lot of dust and pretend they were working very hard. The right system will expose such a person. If you are a good employee, you should have a sense of relief that good performance is being noticed, because it is being documented. A good system is one that encourages employees to become involved in improving their work area and processes.

I had been looking for a top pre-press manager for our company to take us further up the road on our mission. I came down to several choices; however, I had one person in mind. He was the kind of applicant that you know is looking for a great company and not just a job. I decided to show him our systems and how they work by giving him an orientation that demonstrated our system before asking him to make a final commitment. After the orientation and taking him on a tour of our facility, he took the job. Again, the system sold the company—*this time to an employee*—and I didn't have to make any promises and exaggerate our good points and downplay our weak points. We are who we say we are!

I remember a printer that asked me one day to come over to his shop to help set up one of his presses. I got to his shop and started to set up his machine, but to my frustration I couldn't find any tools to work with. I asked the owner, "How do you expect me to set up this machine with just these few broken tools?"

He said that the reason he didn't have any tools was that his employees lost (or took) them and he wasn't going to buy more. I went over to the sink to wash my hands and all he had was a bar of plain soap to remove the ink. At our company, we use a special hand cleaner for removing ink that costs $70 a gallon. I went to dry my hands and he had no paper towels. I had to use the shop towels I had just been using on the press. This owner has complained to me many times that he can't find good employees. I wonder why! This guy is losing a dollar, trying to save a dime. If you have this mind set, you will likely never achieve a great organization and a peaceful environment. You are saying to your employees, "You are not important!"

For our employees, we have a break room at our business that is fixed up like a 1950s diner. It has a lot of nice tables and booths and it also has great memorabilia from the 1950s. When I built this for the employees, I had several managers tell me this was "overkill" and that the employees would not take care of it . . . and, in fact, they would abuse it. I didn't believe that would happen and it hasn't. The employees really enjoy it, because they feel like they have "left the building" when they go there for lunch or a break. It's fun to select a few 1950s tunes on the old Seeberg wall boxes and sit in a booth with your sandwich and a glass of cold Coca Cola. All the amenities are supplied—coffee, assorted candy, ice, napkins, paper plates, plastic forks *and* spoons etc. It's all free. Good employees are worth it!

The laborer is worthy of his reward.
1 Timothy 5:18

CHAPTER 13
WHICH SYSTEM DO I
START WITH FIRST?

THINK OF A ship that's been in battle and has holes everywhere, and water pouring in. Does this sound like any business you know? The best idea is to:

Start With The Biggest Hole First!

In my case, I needed to stop the mistakes in my pressroom, so I built a quality control checklist for the press operators. I will go in depth about this later. The new system stopped a lot of leaks.

Then I went to the next hole and set up a checklist for entering jobs into production, and so on down the line, until I had stopped all the major leaks. To keep the improvement process moving forward, I needed a system to find small and almost undetectable leaks. I searched for a system that would catch these problems that most companies would never find, much less fix. Ah! *The System Buster*—the leak detector. We'll get there later!

Okay, Let's Build the System

Things to consider and build into your system:

Context

The words you use must plainly describe the actions and activity to be performed so that any member of your organization can easily understand. The following story should demonstrate what I mean . . .

The General and the Private

It was told to me that during the Civil War, a famous southern general had a certain private that was stationed right outside his tent. The private was a soldier of below-average intelligence. To be blunt, he wasn't the sharpest tool in the shed. Well, when the general would write out specific orders that would be sent to the front lines, he would call this private in to read the orders. He would then have the private to tell him what they meant, in the private's own words. If the private had any trouble understanding what the general had written, the general would take the orders back to his tent and rewrite them. He would repeat this process until the private could easily explain to him what his orders stated. The general knew that if this private could understand his orders, then, when his officers on the front lines received the orders, they would surely understand them.

As I have stated before, on a scale of one-to-ten, regarding an employee's ability, if someone is a five, then with a great system they can become as effective as an eight or a nine. That's the power of a great system.

Roadie Proof

Here comes another story. I just can't help myself! It's about the days when I played in a rock 'n' roll band—with long hair and shiny clothes.

We had a PA System that was very elaborate. It had many powerful amplifiers that hooked up to lots of speakers, microphones, etc. If the wrong cable was plugged into the wrong speaker, it would blow the speaker. For a civilian, that means it would ruin the speaker. We had a couple of roadies for a while that would help set up our equipment. We were barely scratching out a living and the roadies were probably living with their parents and had not yet learned the art of decision-making.

Well, as fate would have it, one of these roadies plugged in a cable from a 1000-watt amplifier to a speaker that was rated to handle about 200 watts. Yes, it blew up! Being the resourceful and handsome young bandleader that I was, I decided to fix this problem myself. Truth is, there was no money for these kinds of mistakes. Truth is, I wasn't quite as handsome as I thought I was, either! Anyway, I went to an electronic store and bought four different types of cable ends. We wired one cable with one type and the next cable with another type, and so on. It was now impossible to wire a cable to the wrong speaker. It just wouldn't fit. You know, like putting a square peg in a round hole. So, I coined a phrase, "Roadie Proof," that stuck, and people remember when I am explaining how a system needs to be set up, so it would be almost impossible to mess up something. Now my employees know exactly what I mean when I say we need to "Roadie Proof" this or that situation.

Participation

Before a system is set up you should let everyone, whom this system or document will affect, share their ideas about it so they know how it will impact their job. These same people should also be involved in the testing, revising and updating of the system.

Standardization

All references and terms should be used the same way, every time. For example, don't call something in one system or form a cell phone and in the next line call it a mobile phone. When you have hundreds of terms it can get very confusing. Be consistent.

Completeness

There must be no information, logic, or design gaps. Here is an *example* of a complete system and how a complete system works:

A System for Ordering Materials or Supplies so Each Department Never Runs Out

Each person in each department, in fact all employees, should have a daily routine checklist—a list of everything an employee normally does each day.

We will place on the checklist, an entry with a check box beside it to remind them to order materials:

> ❏ *Materials have been ordered and the material order form has been placed in the designated location.*

Every department has a material order form that has listed on it every item used on a regular basis in that department or work area. On this material order form there will be a description of the product, product number, how much to order, etc. The only thing you—any staff member—is required to do is to go down the list of items on this form and put a check in the box beside the item you want to order and place the form in a designated box. *Easy!*

Now, the purchasing person will pick up the material order form and order your materials that day, because the purchasing person has an entry on their daily routine checklist to do so. They won't have to look for the description, the product number, or how much to order, because all the information they need is already on the material order form.

Have you ever gone looking around your building for thirty minutes or more for an old box with the description of the product you need because no one knows exactly what to call it or the product number? This is lost time and money.

Finally, your materials will be delivered to your department or you will be notified that they are in the building ready for you to pick up, because it's on *another person's* daily routine checklist to do so. Now, do you see how one system works with and can affect another system? A system should be designed to be easy to use and work consistently but, most importantly, it must be complete, like a complete circuit. The easier it is to use, the more consistently people will use it.

Understanding

Everyone using a system should understand the meaning of every word and sentence in the system they use.

A manager should know every word and sentence in every system in their department.

The facility manager or owner should know every word and sentence in the entire system unless the organization is so large their position is broken down into several positions.

I was having our online bill of lading system built for our *System100*. As I was reading all the information and looking at the different boxes on the bills of lading from several freight lines we used, I realized I didn't know the use of a particular box that I was to check off. I asked our shipping manager to explain what this box was on the form, and they couldn't tell me. I decided to call one of the freight lines and ask them what the box on the form was and what it meant. They couldn't tell me either—*and it was their form.* I called other freight lines and got the same answer and no one could tell me what it meant or why the box was there. One company put me in touch with their legal department as I wanted to make sure that the form we were drafting was acceptable to them, and I wanted to know what that dumb box was. The legal department could not explain why it was there and in fact joked about it.

The moral of this story? Know each word and sentence in your system.

Compliance

There needs to be a way to follow up on systems to insure that a system is being used and used properly. We have several follow-up systems. See System Buster on page 79.

Un-Losable

Come up with a way to connect or reference the system/ document to other often-used documents that will guarantee it will not be forgotten. "Out of sight, out of mind" is true! As we were building our operations manual, we found that we would need a policy or a procedure to correct something, only to find out later we already had that policy or procedure—we had simply forgotten about it. This happened several times, and it was very frustrating. Even though we are constantly updating our operations manual, there are those forms or systems that are used for specific situations and only come around once a year.

I was going over some of the systems with a new manager, and he asked if we had a particular system in place. I told him we didn't, but we could easily implement one. I had him draw up a rough draft of what he wanted, and had someone lay out the document.

As we started talking to other people in the company to see how this new system would affect other systems, somebody said, "Hey, we already have that system." Well, I went back to my office even more frustrated, but decided right then and there we would try to reference every system document we had to other relative system documents. Since every system document has a form number and a name, it was easy to start implementing. I just looked at this as continual improvement for our operations manual.

Through wisdom a house is built and by understanding it is established. By knowledge, the rooms are filled with all precious and pleasant riches.
Proverbs 23:31

Operations Manual, Departments, Forms Management

I like to use D-Ring binders for each department. Each form will be placed in a sheet protector for easy removal when copying and updating. If your company is very small or you are just starting a business or organization, you could start with one large D-Ring binder and have tabs for each department until it becomes too full, then you can break out each department with its own binder.

I would suggest using no more than three or four fonts on your documents. We use Arial for content, Arial Black for headings,

Aachen for headings, Zapf Dingbats BT for checkboxes and other symbols. Helvetica or Times are also good fonts to use. Remember, standardization is the name of the game in your operations manual. I recommend that all of your forms and documents be built in Microsoft Word. Your supply list and master list of forms for your operations manual should be built in Microsoft Excel. However, if it is a very complicated form, you may consider other design programs.

All companies have common departments, even if you are a very small operation—sales, human resources, accounting departments, etc.

The first page of each department's D-Ring binder should be a list of the forms or documents for that department, built in Microsoft Excel. This should also be placed in a plastic protector sheet.

This compiling and organizing of documents and forms into an operations manual is called forms or document management.

Now give each document a code or form number, along with a revision date. Example: **YCI-HR-0019 Rev 09/04** or possibly:

YCI=Your Company Inc.
HR=Human Resource Dept
0019=number you assign to that document
Rev=Revision Date **09/04**

If you have a better way of doing this, great! I would suggest you put zeros in front of your numbers in the event you sort them in Excel, they will line up. They will also line up when you name your files and store them in a folder on your hard drive. We have a folder for each department.

Example: 009, 010 and *not* 9, 10 etc. Do a test by sorting your forms in Microsoft Excel and you will see what I mean. See pictures of our operations manual along with forms in back of book.

Job Descriptions

An organization or business should have a detailed job description—a list of specific tasks and responsibilities—for each and every position or person, including the owner. Some job descriptions may include several positions. In smaller companies, one person may wear a lot of "hats!"

When we started building our operations manual, we had only four or five job descriptions for our company. One description heading was Press Operator *and* Bindery Operator; another was Delivery Driver *and* Bindery Operator, etc. You just keep breaking them down as you grow.

Daily Routine Checklist

This document is a job description that is broken down into a checklist of every task or duty a person does from the time they arrive at work until the time they leave. This is a great tool for a company's system. With this document, you have at your fingertips a list of everything an employee does. You don't have to ask someone else what a particular employee does or try to remember it yourself. All you have to do is pick up their daily routine checklist and read what they do. This can be very helpful when one of your employees tells you they have too much to do. If you agree they have too much to do, since your business may be growing, it's easy enough to look at their daily routine checklist and make a decision to give a certain task or duty to someone else. Just add, delete or exchange a task from one daily routine checklist to another. The task may be a better fit for someone else, or for someone who doesn't have as much to do.

You see the daily routine checklist gives you eyes to see every task and duty performed in your organization . . . from taking the mail to the post office, to mopping the floors.

If you have twenty or more employees, you could bring all the daily routine checklists for a certain department, lay them out on a table and really see who is doing what or who needs to do what. *Systems are your eyes and ears*!

One way to start building the daily routine checklists is to have everyone in your organization write down everything they do. And I mean *everything*! You will be greatly surprised at how much some people do and how little others do. You will also find out that some people are doing the same task as another person, only at different times. This is an easy fix. Have one person do the task all the time, if possible. Remember: this is *standardization*. You will see with this system how easy it is to *get everything in your organization done every day, every time!*

Let me give you an example of how detailed our checklists have become.

I had a tape player that played music while callers were on hold. It would shut itself off every week or so. Well, I wanted it playing all the time, right? But I either had to remember to check it myself or put it on someone's daily routine checklist:

☐ *Music On Hold player is working.*

I did that, and it was checked every morning, until I improved the system by buying a player that didn't shut off. Continual improvement!

This may seem to be a small thing. But several "small" things can often add up to big frustrations! Imagine having hundreds to thousands of things, getting done every time, every day. Your business starts to run like a well-oiled machine. With these things being done automatically, a more peaceful atmosphere starts to emerge. People can do their job without the constant intervention of others.

Quality Control or Service Control Checklists

These types of checklists are crucial to any company that wants to guarantee quality and service.

You may not be a manufacturer, but every company and organization has a product it is selling or promoting to a customer. Your product may be a service, but it should be quality service.

I have been asked many times by service organizations, "Why does *our* business need the same kind of controls as a manufacturer? What about our *commitment* to quality and service?"

I tell them, "I don't care how committed you are; without a checklist system, you cannot guarantee or prove quality or service, because you are human and you can't remember every process consistently.

Remember the company president I mentioned earlier, who said, "We don't need good systems, we just need good people" Think about this statement for a moment. Aren't you glad that the airlines don't think that way? Before trained, professional pilots *(good people)* take off and land, they use a *checklist.* They know that all it takes is one time to forget to do something—like put down the wheels before landing—and many people will die.

After having a lot of success in my own company with checklists, I wondered why hospitals didn't have one person going down a simple checklist before a surgeon starts to operate. You have probably heard horror stories of the wrong leg being cut off, etc. Well, thank God, the good hospitals are now doing just that. Checklists! Yes, the doctor is a *trained professional,* but with a checklist it is almost impossible that he will operate on the wrong leg.

A Checklist Never Forgets

When you use a checklist properly, the list of entries on the checklist is to be completed *one entry or item at a time.* When one entry is completed, it is checked off as completed. You don't do all the tasks or items on a checklist, and then go down the list checking them off as "completed." By the same token, you don't check off everything on the checklist first, and *then* go about doing the tasks by memory. If you do that, you are gambling with the results. The checklist is used to focus your attention on one thing at a time.

Have you ever read something and it turns out that you have read it *wrong*? Or, you were supposed to do something and it turns out you didn't, but you "just knew" you had? I have! That is because we are human and we don't see things, or do things, the same way every time. Our mind may be focusing on many things, or something major, and miss something small. The airline pilot could be focusing on the weather or passengers and miss a small light that alerts him as to whether his landing gear is up or down. Checklists are not for "dummies," but for busy, normal human beings who simply can't remember everything about everything all the time. Checklists make the necessary details a no-brainer!

The First Day We Used the Checklist System

A fond memory I have is the first day we used the checklist system. True story. There were a lot of skeptics and naysayers when we first began to develop the checklist system. I wanted to start using them in the pressroom first. On day one, I walked out into the pressroom with the first checklist and gathered everyone in production around a light table for a demonstration of how to use a checklist. I had the press operator set up a job and get ready for approval with the new checklist. Well, he set up the press, made all his adjustments and when he was ready to start printing the rest of the job (we were printing letterheads at the time), he brought it over to me to be approved. I took the new checklist and picked up the digital job ticket for printing the letterhead and started to check off.

The first item on the checklist was:

❑ *Color of ink correct*

I looked at the letterhead and then looked at what the job ticket called for. It was correct. I made a check in the box by the item.

Next item read:

❑ *Paper type correct*

I looked at the letterhead, looked at what the job ticket called for and it was correct, so I put a check by it.

Next item read:

❑ *Color of paper correct*

The job ticket called for a *gray color paper* and I looked at the color of paper we were about to print and it was *cream color paper*. We had the *wrong* color of paper and we were about to print 10,000 letterheads. You should have seen the look on everyone's faces. Yes! The very first time we used a checklist, it saved a job from having to be reprinted and having a very unhappy customer—not to mention the extra expense. I didn't have to convince anybody that a checklist is *not* a waste of time. I believe it was the providence of God, as we were starting out with our first quality control checklist. And it worked. As a matter of fact, the person running the press that day is now one of the strongest supporters we have for the checklist system. His reruns due to errors (jobs that have to be reprinted) have almost gone to zero. Thousands of dollars and hours have been saved with checklists. They are one of the keys to our success.

Some people welcome checklists, while others are insulted by them. Apparently, they believe they are they are just too smart to make a dumb mistake. But it happens to the best of us! No matter what anyone thinks about checklists, they work. It's been proven.

Suggestions for Building a Checklist

Start with the subject, when possible. Example: Instead of a description that says:

☐ *I took the mail to the post office*

Start with the subject, e.g.:

☐ *Mail taken to post office*

You don't need to use "I" in a checklist (example "I did this" or "I did that"). Starting with the subject makes a checklist easier to read and follow.

System Driver

Here's a system that we've come up with that is most likely to be used by manufacturers.

We have a system for our job tickets/job jackets that is unique from others I have seen. For most manufacturing facilities, the *job jacket* is used just to hold information such as samples, proofs, etc. That's part of the order. It is also used to hold the *job ticket*—the specifications needed to manufacture a job, such as size, type, color etc. What we have discovered and implemented is the use of the *job jacket* itself as a *"driver"* of the system.

This is a checklist that contains the necessary steps for the entire manufacturing process printed right on the job jacket. You could call it a *CHECKLIST OF ALL CHECKLISTS.*

It starts with *data entry* items that need to be checked, all the way to *shipping* items that need to be checked. As we move down the driver, and we come to an item or process that has its own checklist, we simply refer to that other checklist.

Example of an Item Listed on the Driver:

❑ *Pressroom quality control checklist **(BEY-PD-543)** has been completed, signed, stapled to a press sheet and placed in the job jacket*

[Note: We also reference the form number of the quality control system. We have found the more places we can reference a system within another system, the more likely that it will be used consistently and will not get lost. See *Un-Losable* on page 67].

Due to space constraints on the job jacket, you may not be able to place every item that needs to be checked on the driver. You must decide if an entry or item needs to be on the driver or on its own special checklist, like the example above. The "driver" system is a great way to see at a glance that all quality *and* service control checklists have been completed without opening the job jacket and looking for each quality *and* service control checklist. It is also a picture or flowchart of your manufacturing process from beginning to end.

Policies

Webster's Dictionary says, "A policy is prudence in the conduct of affairs; a course of administrative actions." As I have already stated in this book, you must take the time, be prudent and write things down so your employees don't have to guess what actions they should take, or not take, in various situations. We have even used policies to exempt certain procedures in certain situations. Instead of telling your employees to try and remember under which circumstances they should or should not do something, write it in a policy and it becomes part of the system.

When writing some policies, you don't always need to re-invent the wheel or start from scratch. There are many places to find written policies to give you a good starting point to customize them for your organization. You can find them on the Internet, especially Human Resource documents such as employee handbooks, etc.

A policy should reflect your mission statement and your code of ethics. This is why I strongly recommend you read your mission statement and code of ethics often.

There is also information on the Internet that will teach you how to write a policy. But if you just use common sense, it will take you a long way in your writing of policies. Now, in your employee handbook, you need to be careful and not write anything that is unlawful, and be sure to mention somewhere in your employee handbook that it is not a contract. You may look on the Internet for other pitfalls in writing employee handbooks and other policies.

Procedures

I have learned to really appreciate procedures, as they really are great time savers—which mean they make money. When you think of procedures in that way, in that they make money and empower people to do their job with less direct supervision, you, too, will come to appreciate them. Think how many times someone has come into your office and asked you if you would show them *again* how to do a certain task. They say they forgot, but why should they remember, when they have you as a living, walking and talking computer/procedure. They use the excuse, "Well, I just don't do that task everyday and I just can't remember how to do it." So, you stop what you are doing and spend the time showing them again and again and again. Then just when they finally get it, they leave the company and you start over again, training the next person. This is where a good time saving procedure comes in. Take the time to write a procedure so that anybody can follow it.

Remember we talked about the "general and the private" and how to "roadie proof" a system?

You will only have to write it once and it becomes part of the operations manual. After writing the procedure, go through the steps in the procedure step-by-step, while actually performing the task, to find the holes. Once you are satisfied that you have found the holes and corrected them, have someone else use the procedure (while you are watching them) to see if they stumble over your words or if there is a missing step. Correct all problems until you know they can do it without you. The next time someone asks you again to show them how to do a task, simply hand them the procedure. To really complete this system, the new procedure should be made accessible to them so you can, at that point, just refer them back to the system. Now, as you get better writing procedure, you can then train others how to write them.

Can you see a little clearer, how working on your business is making you profit?

*Then the LORD said to Moses, "Come up to Me
on the mountain and be there; and I will give you tablets
of stone, and the law and commandments which I have
written, that you may teach them.*
Exodus 24:12

CHAPTER 14
OTHER TYPES OF SYSTEMS THAT TRANSFORM AN ORGANIZATION

The System Buster - The Leak Detector

This system is actually a form, and is used as a tool to eliminate internal disorder and mistakes. This has been *THE most important system used to transform our company.* When we're not dealing with chaos and disorder in our own organization, we have more time to serve and educate our customers.

The System Buster is a system used to identify or find "non-conforming events" in your system so you can fix the system, which will in turn *fix* your problems. A non-conforming event signals that a system—procedure, checklist, chain of command, etc.—is not being followed. It can also be an event *not* found in the system because it has never been added to the system via a checklist or procedure, etc. A *non-conforming event* will *bust* or throw a wrench in the gears of the system. Therefore, I named the system the "System Buster." With the thought of having a little fun, I also wanted it to be memorable. I even put a cartoon of a cop handing out a ticket on the System Buster form for impact, because when someone fails to adhere to the system, it's like someone running a red traffic light. You should get a ticket. If we didn't have traffic lights, imagine the chaos and disorder. A traffic light is a system that keeps us from running into each other. How many times do we run into each other and cause wrecks and disorder in our company because someone fails to follow the system? (See sample of document on page 126.)

We are very serious about the System Buster system. It has been one of the most powerful systems that I have ever seen in operation. *It tries the system and demands a verdict.*

System Buster Will Literally Transform an Organization!

We have fixed hundreds of problems with this system. *Fix* is the key word here. Most companies put a bandage on a problem to patch it temporarily, but they rarely fix it so it doesn't happen again.

Example of a Non-Conforming Event

If there was a check box on my daily routine checklist to check my materials inventory to make sure I had enough materials to do my job, and I failed to actually perform the task, but checked it off as though I had done it—I have *busted the system*. In short, I lied to the system. Consequently, the job has to be put on hold until the purchasing person can order and pick up the needed supplies. The error has stopped production, cost the company time and money, and caused disorder, because I was non-conforming.

Remember, a system is like a circuit on a circuit board. This non-conforming event just shorted out the circuit—another example of one system affecting another system.

When a non-conforming event occurs, the System Buster is issued in a similar way a traffic ticket is issued. We fill out the System Buster by first identifying and stating what happened. In this case, you would state on the form the name of the person who failed to order supplies. We then determine if it is a *system error* or a *personal error*—the only two reasons something goes wrong inside our organization.

1. Personal Error. This is where a person fails to follow the system, like the example above. We generally call the person or persons together and ask them what happened. The usual response is, "I was in a hurry, so I really didn't follow the checklist properly." We then remind the employee of the reasons we have the checklist and that checking off an event as completed when it is not, is falsifying the checklist. At our company, we take this seriously and we let them know this type of behavior is not acceptable. We have them sign the System Buster and then we move on. If an employee gets more System Buster's due to personal errors we put them in their employee file and, if the grievance is warranted, we fill out a disciplinary form. You will know right away if an employee is going to adhere to the system or try to play the system. With the System Buster, you can't play the system.

At this point, you may be thinking that this is all pretty harsh. But that is not the intent. If you're going to build a good system, everybody needs to be *on* the system. We give grace when grace is due, and over the years we have only had to fill out a few disciplinary forms. When people realize we are going to adhere to a system, they either embrace the system or they quit. This is an excellent follow-up system to all of your systems, and when employees know the system is being followed up and followed through, you will have compliance.

2. System Error. This is where an event occurs, causing problems or a mistake because it was never incorporated into the system due to the fact it was never encountered before. The event is not found or discussed on any checklist, procedure, policy or any written system. Therefore, the *blame goes to the system, not the person*. At that point, we meet with those people who were affected by the system failure to find out whether this is a *preventable event* or a *non-preventable event*. If it's found to be a *preventable event*, we brainstorm until be find a way to incorporate it into the system and then update the system so this event doesn't happen again. Everyone that was involved with this System Buster signs the document.

If it's found to be a *non-preventable event* then the *blame still goes to the system*. However, we know it can't be prevented because it was either:

An Act of God. Example: lightning striking your power grid and you miss a deadline, or,

A mistake made by your customer in which they gave you wrong information.

When the customer makes the mistake, *they* pay to have the work redone. We can't prevent these types of events with our system; however, we have some emergency plans for Acts of God, and educational tools for our customers to help them reduce their errors.

You may want to give all of your customers this book. You could use it as an educational tool to show your customers how you eliminated most of your errors and chaos.

Now, do you see that after many years of using the System Buster it can turn an organization into a powerful machine that delivers great quality and service? Your internal chaos can be almost totally eliminated.

The System Buster allows everyone in the company, to be involved in correcting and improving the system. If a person fails to follow the system and it hinders someone else's workflow, then the person who has been hindered can issue a System Buster. They are doing the "busting." They become the "cop," helping to identify where the traffic violations are occurring. So then we can fix it as a team. Our staff has actually had fun with this system. The idea is not to place blame or tattle on another employee, but for the purpose of continual improvement.

Yes, there will be people who are personally offended when they have to sign a System Buster. But again this is where leadership and training comes in. You see, an excellent system exposes good and bad behavior or habits. Because it's all coming down to the truth: "Yes, I will follow the system," or "No, I won't follow the system."

I had a customer service person (I will call her Martha) come into my office one day to go over some System Busters that named her as the reason for a certain problem. She told me that she was growing tired of these System Busters and she thought we were going too far because she had never worked in a business that had a system like this.

I said, "Martha, how far do you think we should go in trying to fix problems at our company? Do you think we should get 80 percent of the problems fixed and not worry about the rest?"

She said, "No!"

I said, "Well, how about us fixing 90 percent of the errors or problems—would that be good enough, even though the 10 percent we don't fix may affect the person in the next department and make their job more difficult?"

She said, "No!" Then to my amazement she said, "How about 98 percent!" But, no sooner had she said that, she paused, lowered her head and said, "You can't! You can't stop at 98 percent! You have to try and fix everything!" She signed the System Busters without any more complaining.

We also have a system that is almost identical to the System Buster system except it is used to track how many reprints we have on jobs due to errors. We call it the *Reprint Due to Error System*. We have had this system in place for years to measure our success in improving our production system. We have gotten our reprints-due-to-errors to less that one half of one percent, and some months we have had *zero* reprints due to error. The System Buster is used to track and measure all other internal processes in our business.

A System to Change the System

Yes, you also need a system to change the system! (See sample of Forms Change/Update document on page 127.)

I will never forget the time I wanted to quit and give up on this system stuff. It was the day when one of my customer service representatives came into my office and told me a job was not printed right and the customer was not happy. So I asked what had happened to cause the error. When I was told, I was devastated. I said, "We had that error happen just last week and I know we fixed the system by updating the pressman quality control checklist that addressed that error!" So I went out to the pressroom and grabbed a checklist. The update I had personally made was not on it. I asked the pressman, "Where is the new checklist I gave you last week?"

He said, "I put the *new checklist* in the rack along with the *old checklist* because I didn't want to waste paper."

I said, "Don't you understand, when we change a checklist the old ones need to be thrown away? I don't care about saving a few pennies worth of paper." Using an old checklist can cost hundreds or thousands of dollars. Well, it was not his fault; it was mine!

Edward Deming says if you don't give your employees the right tools and the time to do their job then don't blame them for the results. A system is a tool. I went back to my office to have a pity party, and thought of giving up on these systems, but it only lasted about ten minutes and then the light bulb came on—we need a System to Change the System.

I went to work building the checklist system for changing and updating our forms. One of the items on the checklist was:

❑ *All old copies of this form have been thrown away in every location.*

Well, it's working today, and we haven't had that problem show up again. The fact of the matter is, ISO had a similar system for a while; I just didn't know it existed. But it shows you that these systems are really universal and every type of organization runs into a lot of the same issues.

Whoever loves instruction loves knowledge,
but he who hates correction is stupid
Proverbs 11:1

Recap of Building a System

A. Determine if a system needs to be built

    1. *Unpredictable events* - no reason to build system

        • Outside disruptions - clients, vendor, Acts of God

    2. *Predictable events*

        •The event is not in the system but the event *can* be predicted therefore *we build a system*

B. Fix the "biggest hole" first - prioritize those systems that are most critically in need of change

C. Examined the current system. Don't employ the "if it ain't broke, don't fix it" rule until you have examined the current process in light of the bullet items in Step E

E. Assign a staff member or group—the ones that will be affected by the process to *create a new system* or *improve a currently running system*. Make changes to old system only if it:

      • Stops errors and chaos

      • Streamlines the process

      • Standardizes the process

      • Saves time and/or cost

F. As you begin to design or improve a system:

    1. Note all personnel involved in that process

    2. Write down the process step-by-step as you think it would make the most sense

    3. Think about the flow of the process and how each step effects the next step (from who/what to who/what, etc.) *Roadie proof the process*

    4. Create a step-by-step checklist, procedure, policy or form *(Remember standardization of terms)*

    5. Call a meeting or pass the document to each person effected by this system

    6. Each person should review each step in the process *(looking*

for gaps or holes), give their input as to whether it will work and if they understand every word *(General and the Private)* or what needs to be changed or revised

7. Once various changes have been made in the system, have everyone review again. Repeat steps 6 and 7 until every one is satisfied with the results

8. The System Manager / Head of Organization—should give final approval (see Forms Change/Update on page 127.)

The 100 Percent System of Cleanliness

One hundred percent system is what we call our system of cleanliness. Don't miss this! *If you don't get anything else out of this book, get this!* This was the most surprising system I discovered on my journey to building a great company. It is used to clean and organize all of our hard systems, things like machinery, cabinets, desks, the entire building and grounds etc. I think this system has gotten us more attention and unexpected, positive feedback than any other system we have implemented. The reason is that people get a lasting impression of your business when they see it for the first time.

Truth . . .

You don't get a second chance to make a first impression!

People have a preconceived picture in their mind of what a printing company looks like. So, when they see our offices, bindery, pressroom and warehouses are immaculately clean, it totally takes them by surprise. They expect to see dirty floors with ink stains and paper laying everywhere. But we keep our shop clean for the same reason you dress up to make a good first impression. Your house cleaning is out in the open and cannot be hidden. It's an open statement of who you are. Simply put, the 100 percent system of cleanliness is: *everything in its place and a place for every thing.*

The 100 Percent System in Action

Several years ago, our production manager was very frustrated with Mark, one of my best employees, about his messy work area. I've asked his permission to use his real name. Mark has always been hardworking and very dedicated, but when it came to keeping his work area clean, he was about a two on a scale of one to ten. Our production manager had come to the point of firing Mark and that made me very uncomfortable. I asked the production manager to let me work with Mark and develop a system of cleaning, just for him. As Edward Deming believed, I also believe—If you don't have a system for something then you shouldn't expect people to perform at top levels.

Although we kept a fairly clean facility by then, it was nowhere near "world class," and that's our mission. So, I asked Mark to come into work the following Saturday and Sunday. I told him that he and I would detail clean and develop a cleaning system for his small press department. Before that Saturday arrived, I ordered special cabinets, plastic bins, and a variety of organizational supplies. We already had a great label printer. We started out that Saturday morning cleaning and organizing. We wanted a designated and labeled location for every single item in his department. But, it wasn't going to be just any place; it would be a *well-thought-out-and-planned location*. It had to be convenient. Everything needed to be in an easy-to-clean, permanent and sturdy container (no cardboard). And the container had to look good. We cleaned and scrubbed all day Saturday and Saturday night, then again after church on Sunday and Sunday night. We had that place looking great!

With each item we wanted to organize, I would ask Mark questions like, "Do you use this item on a daily basis, once in awhile, or does this item even belong in your department?" Let me tell you, it took about 120 total man-hours to completely develop this system. I had never cleaned and organized anything in my life to that degree of detail. We were extremely proud of it, so I decided to play a little game.

I asked one of the women in customer service to give Mark and me an inspection. I asked her to see if she could find anything, and I mean anything, no matter how small or seemingly unimportant, that was out of place. I gave her the rules. I told her *every item* had a designated place that should be clearly labeled and that it should be in a permanent container that looked good. Well, she did her inspection and, being a detailed person, she found a plastic bin that wasn't labeled and one paper clip lying behind a light table. Yes, one paper clip. That's the kind of inspection I was looking for. So I labeled the bin and found the place where the other paper clips were located, and put the one paper clip in its place. I heard comments from other employees and the production manager like, "Yeah, but will it stay clean?" I wasn't really sure.

I told Mark at the end of his workday, all he needed to do was put *all* the items he used back in their designated place, just like he was filing papers. I asked him to come and get me after he put everything up for the day, and I would do an inspection. At the end of the day, I went to inspect his department and it looked great! I did notice a T-square lying across the light table and I noticed some paper strips lying on top of the plate camera. I also saw a few items that were not placed in the designated location we had decided they should be.

I said, "Mark, the T-square has a hook for you to hang it on."

He said, "Oh, yeah, I forgot the hook." And he hung it up.

Then I looked around and said, "What are all those paper strips lying around?"

He said he used them for masking out certain images on the camera.

I also asked, "Why are these other items not in the designated location we agreed to put them?"

He said, "Well, when I started working, I realized they weren't in a convenient place."

So right then, together, we found a more convenient place for the items he had moved. I went and got a plastic tray and labeled it MASKING SHEETS for those loose strips of paper. The next day, we repeated the inspection process and very few adjustments were made to our new cleaning system. The following day I came out for my inspection and his department was at what I call 100 percent. Every item, *down to a paper clip,* was in its designated place. From then on, it stayed between ninety-eight and 100 percent. I can't tell you how proud and amazed I was at this discovery and how simple it was.

One day after Mark had gone home, I asked the production manager who had wanted to fire Mark, and another manager, to come and see the small press department. I asked them this question: If they had walked into this department and didn't know the person who was working there . . . on a scale of one to ten, as far as cleanliness and organization is concerned, what would they rate that person? They both agreed, "A nine or a ten." But I said, "Since you know Mark, what is his rating, really? They both said, "A two or a three." You see, with a good system, a two became a nine.

Since then, we have put that 100 percent system to work at every desk, every department, and in every area of our company. Again, we are following the mission statement of adhering to a system of cleanliness.

With the 100 percent system in place, if an item is out of it designated place, it sticks out like a sore thumb. It's very easy to inspect. In fact, as soon as you walk into a room you can see an item out of place. This makes managing easy. If you had a old beverage can sitting out in a room that was perfectly in order you would notice it right away, but if you had the same beverage can sitting in a room full of junk you wouldn't even notice it.

Let's Recap the 100 Percent System Rules . . .

It is a system that is everything has a designated and labeled location and everything is in its location.

Not *80 percent* of things, but *100 percent* of all items we use will have a designated location. And at the end of the shift or day, all items go back in their location.

It sounds simple and it really is. However, most companies—especially manufacturing companies—are usually not very clean and organized due to a very simple fact, they really don't have a *system of cleaning.* Now, they may straighten things up and some may even have a maintenance crew clean the offices, but I'm talk-

ing about a system that covers every area of the organization—
Every department, *every* desk, *every* cabinet, *every* machine, *every*
table—not one thing is unaccounted for in the 100 percent system.

Why the 100 Percent System Works

Let's say we started the day with our workstation or desk some-
what in order. As the day goes along, we use more and more of our
work materials and our workstation or desk becomes more cluttered.
I'm sure you've seen people's workstation or desk looking like
someone took a trashcan and emptied it on top. You've seen whole
departments looking as if a bomb had gone off in them. This is
chaos!

So when we can't stand the mess anymore, we begin to
straighten things up a bit. Place a stack of stuff here and a stack of
papers there. This may look better, it may *look* clean and organized,
but this is *not* organization. This is just straightening up, because the
next day when you straighten up, some items may be in a totally different place.

You may say, "Why does this matter?" Well, it matters because
you can't be sure where every item is, especially when you're using
lots of items. If a person has to work behind you, it may take hours
for them to find something. Everyone should be able to find every
item in your work area, effortlessly, and especially you! Everyone
should know exactly where the scissors are—not probably, but
exactly where everything should be—because it is labeled and has a
designated place. Sometimes you may have one plastic bin for just
one item, such as a flashlight. You may say this is overkill, but it
works! The closer we get an area to 100 percent, the more time and
money we save, because it doesn't take minutes, and in some cases
hours, to find things. How many times have you gone looking for
something in your business . . . something as simple as a flashlight
. . . and it took an hour or more to find it? Or, you're looking for a
file or a certain piece of paper and it's lost somewhere in the chaos
and it takes you ten or more minutes to find that.

Let's talk money. You've heard "time is money," so imagine if
you had a big glass bowl and every time you or someone in your

organization looked for something and couldn't find it, you tore off a small piece of paper and wrote on it the time it took to locate an item and how much money that time cost. After a year how full do you think that bowl would be? We have saved bowls and bowls of minutes of time over the past ten years.

What are some of the other benefits besides saving thousand of minutes in your business?

When our outside cleaning service comes to vacuum, sweep, dust, mop, etc., at the end of the day, they don't have to straighten up and move everything out of the way before they can clean. More time and money saved; and they can do what they do best, clean your business.

Our outside cleaning service is a very important part of our system. They like to participate in the improvement of our company, because they see how serious we take the cleaning system. That is their business, and they want to be a part of a business that understands *their* business. We have become a model place for them. They actually enjoy cleaning our company because when they are finished it looks great—like a show place!

So What's the Big Deal?

We know the 100 percent system means: Every item has a designated and labeled place, and every item is in its place. If 80 percent of your items had a place and 20 percent of the items didn't have a place, we could call this an 80 percent system. You say, "Well, there are just a few items that don't have a place, so what's the big deal?"

Ah, but after awhile what takes place is, some of the 80 percent starts getting lost in the 20 percent and the system begins to break down into chaos. That's why 100 percent works every time, day after day, month after month, *but any system less than a 100 percent will start to break down.*

Can you imagine an engineer saying, as long as 80 percent of the circuits are in place your television or DVD or computer should work great? No, it works great because 100 percent of the circuits are in place.

Another great thing about this system is, *you only have to build it once*—as long as you get it to 100 percent—and then all you have to do is fine-tune it every now and then.

Our mission statement says, you will be able to witness cleanliness in every area of our company, and you can. *The 100 Percent System is part of our sales and marketing team.* We have won over a lot of potential clients just with a single tour of our facility. Think about this, you may not need to hire that extra sales person. You may just need to implement the 100 Percent System. How much do you pay a new sales person for one year?

Imagine coming into work each day, the floors are immaculate, and everything is in its place, no clutter, and no confusion, which means less stress. Is that not a benefit for you and your employees?

So, Do We Just Clean All Day?

A new pressman we really wanted to hire came in to be interviewed and was shown around our plant. He remarked about its being the cleanest pressroom he had ever seen. He took the job the next day. However, later he related to me that he had gone home to talk it over with his wife and told her how clean everything was. He said he told her he was a little worried because he thought, to be that clean we must not have much work, so he guessed we just clean all day. Nothing could have been farther from the truth!

Our press operators spend little time cleaning the pressroom. With the *100 Percent System*, there is little to do except put the items you worked with that day back in their designated place. And most items are already in their place because the location is so convenient; you naturally put them there as you're working. The outside cleaning service sweeps and mops our pressroom floor every night, and they dust and wipe down the stainless steel workbenches. In most plants, there is so much stuff lying all over the place, managers don't want outside cleaning services touching anything for fear of losing or ruining something.

This new pressman went on to tell me how he showed his daughters our pressroom and the presses he operated and that this was the only company he had worked for where he felt proud to show his family. He said, "Quite frankly, I was ashamed to show them the other companies I worked for." To me this one testimony is worth it all!

> *For God is not the author of confusion, but of peace.*
> 1 Corinthians 14:33

Chart of Accounts - Clearer Vision for Better Decisions

The *chart of accounts* is a list of places (accounts) where your money is spent. Example: office supplies, leases, repairs, payroll, rent, utilities, etc. A chart of accounts is found in all bookkeeping programs, like QuickBooks and other accounting programs. The great thing about having your accounting program set up with a chart of accounts that is customized to your business, is that you can get a daily, weekly, monthly and yearly breakdown and can see where every dollar goes. This is very important for those who have just started businesses, or have been in business for a while. A lot of business owners allow their accountant to totally take care of the chart of accounts . . . or *all* the accounting, for that matter. The problem is, an accountant will use the chart of accounts that he likes, and not necessarily what you *need* to run your business effectively.

A former business owner that was counseling me, said to me, "Philip, you need to have *eyes* for your business!" He told me, the most important thing he had learned from going through losing a couple of businesses was that he didn't fully understand the financial part of business and didn't have his eyes on the numbers to make the right decisions. He said that I needed to set up my own chart of accounts. At that time, I'm almost embarrassed to tell you, I didn't even know what a chart of accounts was. He called PIAS— an association of printers—and had me join. They provided me with a chart of accounts that was customized for a printing company. We then customized my bookkeeping program's standard chart of accounts to match the one from the printing industry. Most industries have a standard chart of accounts already established for their particular industry.

From chart of accounts, you can then get the ratio of certain expenses, compared to your total sales for the month. You may be asking, "Why do I need this ratio and how can I use it?" You can compare it with other people in your industry to see if you may be spending too much money in a certain area.

After the first month of using my chart of accounts to see my expenses, I looked at how much I was spending on paper, which is a very large expenditure for a printing company. I compared it with a book, published by PIAS, of all the printers in my area. It was broken down by profit leaders, and the rest of the printers, as to the ratio of expenses they spend on materials and labor, compared to total sales. I looked in that year's ratio reports and, to my amazement, found I was paying 10 percent more than the profit leaders in my industry were paying. Well, I immediately called in my paper representatives and told them what I had discovered and I got an immediate 10 percent reduction in my price. That one ratio report saved me thousands of dollars. You tell me if your accountant would know that.

You should use your chart of accounts for your "eyes." It will help give you clearer vision to make the right decisions for your company.

Be diligent to know the state of your flocks
and attend to your herds.
Proverbs 27:23

Sales and Marketing Systems
I was surprised to find out that a lot of companies and organizations have no systems or controls for their sales department. They

hire sales people, show them an office, and tell them to, "Get out there and sell something." The only system they have, is to look at their total sales for a given period of time. The problem with only that as your primary tool—and lacking "eyes" to see what the sales person is doing—is that you miss the opportunity to help this sales-person become really successful. You can also lose a lot of money, with this "*fly by the seat of your pants*" system.

I have seen salespeople stay at a company for a year or two, then move to the next company; stay there a year or two, and so on. These sales people know that most companies have no system for tracking their activities, so they get their draw or salary and, essentially, have to answer to know one. It's almost a con game. I really don't think they consider themselves dishonest people, but I believe they know in their heart they put in little effort to get sales; therefore, they are not benefiting the company. On the other hand, if this same person worked for a company that had a sales system, they might flourish. I have interviewed many sales people, and one of the questions I ask an applicant is, "Do you have any system for selling?" The answer is generally very vague or they list some of the things they do to make a sale, none of which would make them very consistent in sell-ing. Again, the old shoot-from-the-hip approach to sales.

I remember a young lady coming in for an interview. I asked her about her system of selling. She had come from a company that had just declared bankruptcy. She said she really didn't have a system, but she was looking for a job. She had been selling for years, going from one company to another, but never achieving any real success. During our interview, she asked me about how we pay, and I said, "Before we talk about pay, I want to know about your sales." After discussing her sales and what she wanted to be paid, it didn't even approach the ratio needed to compensate her. She also informed me she had a few companies competing for her as a sales person. And she has never had to conform to a system of selling. I told her we had a system that would track her calls, appointments and other activities, and she would need to turn in a report each day. She never called back and I probably saved a lot of money.

Companies may have been losing money on this person for years. Yes, you can and will lose money on some sales people even with a system. The good news about a system is, you don't have to lose money on someone for a year or two before you realize this person is not going to work out. When you put someone on a system of selling, you can tell right away if they are working or playing you for their personal gain. Yes, I've been a chump, but my system of selling has saved me money and has helped many sales people to rethink their own "system."

Now, if someone says they will work for commission only, then you know this person is serious about selling. They know that selling on straight commission, if it's a fair percentage, is the path to great money. They don't need you to hold their hand. I've had such a sales person, who was not required to turn in a report. I thought he should have had a system, but I hired him on the premise that he would work out of his house on straight commission. If this person sells—they make money and I make money. If they don't, I pay nothing. Now, if this person were working out of our office along side of other sales representatives, they would have to conform to our system. In one way, this kind of sales person is like contract labor—not much fuss. The reason this even works at our company is that we have such powerful systems of production that a sales person doesn't have to worry about quality or if their customers' jobs go out on time. *I'm happy to say that we are on time, every time about 99.8 percent of the time.* However, I would prefer to have sales people that have a strict system of selling and are constantly looking at ways to improve on their system.

I think it is obvious that you should track the amount of sales a person is doing. In a good sales system, you should also track the amount of suspect calls, prospect calls, and customer calls made each day. You should also track the amount of appointments made, and all this data should be put into a graph to benchmark the results. These appointments and prospects should be used to brainstorm on how to turn these prospects into clients, with the sales person and the owner, or a sales manager, if you have one. You will not believe how even a simple system like this will give you eyes for your sales department, even if you have only one sales person. If you have been running blind, it's been by choice, but you can get some eyes, if you want to. A good system, just like in production or service, is the key to growing a great sales department.

Benchmark Charts for Measuring Growth

It is a great thing to have systems in place; however, when certain systems are introduced, you have to know there will be opposition. But the best way to offset skepticism is to measure your results to see if a system is working. Once you post the results so your people can actually see them, they will be more receptive. People want to see how they are doing on certain tasks.

Remember how anxious you were to get your report card in school at the end of the six-week period? In the same way, our employees look forward to seeing our charts and reports at the end of the month. They actually challenge one another to do better. We have found which systems work through measuring to see if we are improving or not. We have taken down systems where results were minimal and the system was too cumbersome. When your benchmarks at the end of a month look like your heading in the wrong direction, you can address the situation immediately. A lot of companies wait until they are in trouble, then call in an expensive consultant to find out what's wrong; and sometimes, by that time, it's too late. But we have found with our daily approach to systems, like the *System Busters*, we know we are going to get good benchmarks reports, because the whole system is continually being improved on a daily basis.

Projects Management

To help with the transformation in your organization or business, you need a system for administering projects or tasks to people in the organization. This is also where you *must learn* to delegate and train. A project managing system is where you can oversee and watch an organization transforming before your very eyes. This is where you can test the leadership skills of your employees. You are not handing them a complete system that they follow, you are assigning them either a one-time project, like overseeing the installation of a new copier, or it may be you are giving them a task to actually build a system. Leaders will surface here. But like any system, this project system *must have follow-up*.

A leader/manager needs training just like any other employee. Delegate as much as you can without disrupting your employees daily routine. Remember, if you are assigning someone to build a system, you should give the final approval. This means you need to know exactly how the new system works.

You could start your project system with a simple list of tasks in Microsoft Excel, broken down into categories like name of task or project, assigned to who, date, etc., or you could use the automated task system in Microsoft Outlook. We have used both and they both work fine. There are many out there for you to use.

Our own *System100* software has an excellent task system. This is the way many of our improvements are tracked. When someone submits an idea for improvement, it immediately goes into the company projects database and is categorized into one of several different categories and prioritized.

You see, most companies have slow periods, but they don't use the slowdowns very effectively. They don't have a written list of improvements that need to be accomplished, or again these improvements are kept in the owner's or manager's head. When our company or a department has a slowdown, we immediately assign someone a task to accomplish, something that will benefit us. They get paid and, at the same time, the company is improving, we are not just doing busy work.

In our time management software, our employees clock in on "special projects for general manager." This is where the general manager is able to track all company projects. This is how we know how much time we spend on these special projects for a given period. We can create a benchmark, a ratio of *chargeable* work versus *un-chargeable* work. In this way, we can keep it in balance and, if needed, we can even create a budget for time spent on special projects.

Inventory System

Every well-organized business needs to have an inventory of all of its assets broken down into different categories like computer hardware, software, office furniture and decor, machines and tools, office supplies, etc. Businesses lose a great deal of money through theft and misplacement of assets and other materials.

The housekeeping of some companies and organizations is so bad that assets, parts and other materials are constantly being lost due to clutter and junk laying everywhere. In this type of organization, you may buy two of everything—one to use and one to lose. It should be on someone's daily routine to update and make sure all assets and other materials coming in to the organization are added to the inventory. Some inventory software can be found on the Internet at very affordable prices.

Orientation System

A pressman we recently hired told me a story about a well-known printing company here in Nashville, that he'd gone to work for, and how excited he was to be hired. He heard they were one of the best printing companies in our city. After a few weeks he became very disillusioned. The things he had heard were not the things he was experiencing. They didn't give him an orientation so he really didn't have a good picture of whom he was going to work for.

In most companies that don't have an orientation system there are gaps in people's knowledge of the company. It may take years of being employed there, until they really get a picture of the who, what, when, where and why.

Every time we give an orientation, I hear from the new employee how grateful they are to know our history, our vision and a detailed orientation of our systems. They know whom they are going to work for, what to expect, and what is expected of them.

A friend of mine went to work for a company a few years ago, and I later asked him about what the company did, and what his job was, etc. I was amazed that, even after several months, he couldn't really explain their actual business with any clarity. The company was just starting out, had few or no systems, and management was just too busy *doing* to get a handle on, or explain, what each employee should actually *do*.

This is a good example of why there must be a good orientation system. New hires, *and every member of your team*, should be fully briefed on exactly what your company is about; what your Mission Statement is (and what it means); the "chain of command;" what each department does and how they relate to each other; policies and procedures; the what and where of equipment, supplies and tools they will be using—*everything* they need to know to do their job. A detailed orientation system can make the difference as to whether your new employee hits the ground running, or flounders in confusion for a time trying to figure it all out for themselves.

Performance Evaluation

An employee should have an evaluation of their performance. This is a great way to measure, like any other benchmark. Just as the company is improving, so should every employee. It shows the employee where they stand, sort of like a school report card. It's the eyes for management to see what the managers/supervisors think of the people they are managing and supervising. It's a documented system for their employee record.

Story time . . . I had one of my managers—I'll call him Arnold—give an evaluation to the employees in his department. Later, I went over each evaluation and gave them to our human resources department for filing. About six month later, Arnold left on his vacation. While he was gone, I was filling in for him and I was getting a first-hand view of the department and the different people in the department. We also had just installed our new computerized time management system that reported on how long it took to do a particular task. I noticed that a particular person (let's call her

"Sally") seemed very slow in doing her main task. Well, that was the impression I was getting, but as I have stated many times in this book, *you shouldn't go by impressions or feelings.*

So I did the right thing and pulled a detailed report of every job Sally had done for a month. The report said she was taking almost twice as long as she should. I then started to interview various people in the department and they began to unload their burdens on me about Sally. They all confirmed that she was not only slow, but told me of other negative things Sally was doing. I asked each of them if they had reported it to Arnold, the department manager; they *all* said they had. Some also told me in private that they were a little nervous about going around Arnold. I pulled Sally's latest performance evaluation to see how Arnold had evaluated Sally and was surprise to see that Sally had been given very high marks in just about every area of her performance.

After this I put in The Buck Stops Here system and other *follow-up systems* to ensure this didn't happen again.

When Arnold returned from vacation, I gave him a *written* report of everything I had witnessed in his absence and what the employees had shared. Arnold did not have a good explanation, other than to tell me the employees were wrong in their assessment of Sally. *The system* said otherwise, and confirmed what every employee was saying about Sally was true.

As you can see an evaluation is valuable, in more ways than one.

Nearly all men can stand adversity,
but if you want to test a man's character, give him power.
Abraham Lincoln

CHAPTER 15
A LITTLE LAGNIAPPE (EXTRA)

MY FATHER, HENRY Beyer, was from New Orleans, Louisiana and I remember he liked to use the word lagniappe (pronounced lan-yap) when he tried to teach us about doing something a little special for other people. It's a Creole/French term that means "a little extra," like a small present given to someone. So, here's a little lagniappe for those with small or start-up businesses.

Barter or Trade Organizations

Barter or trade organizations are set up for small businesses to find customers that they would not normally have. There are several out there; like BXI and Trade Bank. The way they work is: you become a member for a small start-up fee and they place your business name with all their members. If someone needs your product or service they use *trade dollars* to purchase them. Trade dollars are printed checks with the trade organization's name and information on them. You build up a trade bank account just like you would with real dollars. When you need a product, you call one of the members in the organization to get a price and, if you like the price, you buy with your trade dollars.

There are a couple of things to be aware of:

- You pay sales tax just like you would with real money, unless you're exempt.

- You claim the sales in your accounting just like you would with any other sales.

- Some members in the trade organizations will mark up their products more than what is normal. This is not supposed to happen, as you can get thrown out of the organization for marking up too high but, from what I have seen, this policy is not enforced.

Just like any other purchase you make, you need to be alert. "Let the buyer beware," says the old adage.

I have also found that certain trade organizations may be stronger in one city than in another. Before you join, talk to some of the local members; they can tell you who is strong and who to buy from. Some businesses are members of more than one organization. The strength of the organization depends upon the area director for a town or city. Be careful not to over spend or over sell. If your product takes a lot of hard dollars (real money) to produce, such as labor and materials, be very careful not to sell too much. You can go *on hold*, which means once you get your bank account to a certain figure that you're comfortable with, you can stop selling. A business, such as a hotel or radio station, benefits greatly with trade organization dollars, because it costs them little more to rent a hotel room that would otherwise be vacant, or air-time that would otherwise go unused. When I first started out, I used trade dollars for office furniture, carpet and many other items. It also helped me to establish friendships and to network with people who knew a lot about business.

Buy Cheap, Buy Twice
You have heard this before, but *listen* this time! When you buy a cheap item for your business, or an item that is not of good quality, it will end up costing you more and give you more headaches.

Now, I am not saying you shouldn't look for a bargain. Being a good negotiator can mean the success or failure of a business. Here is an example of what I am talking about . . .

When I put in my 100 percent system of cleanliness, I purchased some cabinets that were made of heavy welded steel and were also attractive. I also bought some of those thin steel cabinets you find at office supply chains and other discount stores. The thin cabinets are easily bent and, if you move them, the doors get warped and won't close properly. I have had to replace, or am in the process of replacing, every one of them. The heavy steel cabinets still look like the day I bought them, other than a few scratches. When we moved to our new facility, we didn't have to take everything out of the cabinets we just put them on a dolly with their contents. Another example of this would be if you have a high traffic area and your carpet is constantly in need of cleaning. Why not consider tile? Yes, tile costs more, but if you buy the right kind of tile, it can last a lifetime. It looks good and it is easily cleaned, unlike carpet. In the long run, you save money and your business looks great.

The Worker is Worth Their Wages

Spending a little more money to add quality is a very difficult decision for all organizations and businesses, especially when you are still a small operation. I have lost some very qualified people because I feared I might not be able to afford them. I remember not hiring someone because he wanted a dollar-an-hour more than I was paying, or thought I could afford. He went on to another company and became a star employee. I heard later through the grapevine that he did the work of two or three people.

When I bought my first large printing press, which was going to cost more than my house, I remember thinking, "How am I going to afford this press and the press operator to run it?" I made the trip to New Jersey where the press was located to inspect and purchase the press. While I was there, I got to spend time with the plant manager who was answering my questions about the press.

He said, "Philip, I would like to give you some advice. When you hire an operator for this press, do not hire someone just because they will work for a few dollars less an hour. Look for a great operator and be ready to pay a top wage—they will earn every dime of it. In fact," he said, "They will make you money!"

But I didn't listen because of fear, and immediately upon returning looked for someone who would work for what I wanted to pay.

I hate to admit this, but that little lesson cost me more than I would like to state in this book. I finally learned that lesson. I was a slow learner. I can also tell you, with much experience under my belt, that great employees do earn their money and they will make you money. They will help you in your mission to build a great organization. But remember, great employees do not replace a great system. You need both to develop a great company.

It's not what you pay a man, but what he costs you that counts.
Will Rogers

The Information Age

Today, we are living in what is called the "Information Age." I suggest you use it, but don't get bogged down with it! I do recommend you read trade publications about your industry or business. These are a source of very valuable information. People in your business are going through the same things you are. Learn from them, look for articles, cut them out, organize them and give them to others in your organization or business. I have been saving articles on sales, service, management, production, TQM, etc., for years. I have used and put into practice a lot of the tips and information I've gleaned from these publications. I find now, after ten years of collecting, a lot of the articles about my industry, and business management, are confirming what we have already implemented or believed to be good business. As you hire new employees, give them access to these tips. Only the very best employees will appreciate these. So, don't get frustrated when some don't take them as seriously as you think they should. The important thing is that YOU take them seriously, because the information from these articles and tips can be used to help you grow your organization.

> *The heart of the prudent acquires knowledge,*
> *And the ear of the wise seeks knowledge.*
> Proverbs 18:15

Pay Your Bills

When I started my company in 1988, I asked my brother, Billy — a business owner in Louisiana — if he had any advice he could share with me, to help me succeed. To my surprise, he said, "Yes, pay your bills! In any business, you will have a lot of money coming through your bank account, but remember that it is not *your* money; it belongs to your vendors, your employees, and many other expenses your business will have. If you start spending that money, you will find yourself in deep trouble, and probably lose the business."

He was right! I have seen many businesses go out of business, not for lack of business, but because the owner was not a good steward. Not only did some of them spend their profit, but also spent the monies that belonged to others.

The first eight or nine months I was in business, I didn't take a dime for myself. Even after that, I only lived on the profit. I made sure my employees and vendors were paid first. This has been very valuable to our business, because when we had to go through some tough times our vendors were behind us all the way. They knew our word was good, and they extended the term I needed to get through and keep production going.

The SBA (Small Business Administration) website says that one of the reasons for business failure is personal use of business funds. You can't get any clearer than that.

Do not say to your neighbor, "Go, and come back,
and tomorrow I will pay you" when you have it with you.
Proverbs 3:28

Embrace Technology

I strongly suggest that if you are just starting a business or an organization, it is crucial that you start by using the technology that is available to you at affordable prices. You should have bookkeeping software such as QuickBooks. I believe if you have four or more employees you should also strongly consider *time-keeping software*, instead of using time clocks with time cards. Time-keeping software can be found on the Internet and will pay for itself; in some cases, in the first few months. In fact, most of the software I've purchased, or had custom-designed, has paid for itself very quickly.

The first week I used my time-keeping software, I asked my pressroom manager if he had noticed anything different since we started the new system. He said he noticed people not going in and out of the smoking area as much as they had been. When we used conventional time cards, employees were sometimes not clocking in and out for all smoke breaks, and were taking more than the two breaks we gave them. But when the time-keeping software was put in place, the plant manager could see from their desk's computer who was clocked in, and on what job they were working. When the employees knew that we knew who was on break or at lunch, that behavior stopped immediately. If you have a lot of employees and they are taking longer or extra breaks, a lot of money and production time can be lost. If you are one of those companies that have been in business for a few or many years, and are still not using a computer for your bookkeeping and other operations, I highly recommend you look into these time saving computer programs.

I know companies that have been in business for thirty years and have no computers at all for the operation of their business. The cost is lost time and information. That, I believe, is *self-inflicted blindness!* It's like using candles instead of light bulbs!

And you shall grope at noonday, as a blind man
gropes in darkness; you shall not prosper in your ways.
Deuteronomy 28:29a

Twelve Pillars of a Great Organization
Determination
Discretion
Faith in God
Flexibility
Humility
Knowledge
Organization
Patience
Relationships
Truth
Wisdom
Wise Counsel

The Cookies and Milk Generation
I seem to have interviewed my share of what I call the "Cookies and Milk Generation," otherwise known as the "Baby Boomers"— *my* generation. Many of us have become a growing population of self-made victims. Lawsuits abound, because *we* are the victims of hot coffee that *we* spill, high-fat fast food that *we* eat, and cigarettes that *we* smoke. Anything *we* have a problem with, including things that might deter us from our self-indulgence—like The Ten Commandments—causes many of us to complain, "I am a victim" or "I'm offended." We pout and whine and say we "deserve" or "have a right to" certain things, even though *we* never earned them.

We are not "Baby Boomers"—we are a generation of babies! And we're teaching our children and grandchildren these childish, foolish and destructive ideas. Am I being too hard on my peers? Certainly, this doesn't apply to everyone in my generation—many have worked hard, and fought and died for the freedoms *we* now have to *be* babies and to express foolish ideas. And I'm not saying that there aren't any true victims out there. But I am saying that in many cases being a victim is by choice. We can choose to be victims; or we can choose to be over-comers.

I say, let's stop blaming others for our problems and *fix* our problems by making positive choices everyday.

One of the heroes of my generation—Jim Morrison of The Doors—was a singer that at one time I wanted to emulate; whose music I was fascinated by and often sang. I recently read a quote by Jim Morrison that said, *"I'm interested in anything about revolt, disorder, chaos, especially activity that appears to have no meaning. It seems to me to be the road toward freedom!"*

Sadly, Jim Morrison died of an overdose of drugs. A life or a company without order is certainly *not* the road to freedom. For Morrison, at least, it was the road to death.

Owners and managers, let's take responsibility for ourselves, our organization, and our families. I've heard many of us whining about how we can't find good employees anymore because a generation's work ethic is childish. I agree, and just stated, that my generation and the current generation is pretty spoiled, but complaining about them is not going to change it. We need to change ourselves and our organization, and then the mature employees out there—and there are some—will be attracted to more mature-thinking companies.

A mature company is one that is not afraid of change; one that embraces the ideas of its workers; one that bases its mission and policies on truth; one that doesn't show partiality to one person over another. It's also one that continually looks for ways to improve and to serve its customers. One that is willing to pay the price to build good systems.

Employees, we need to stop pouting about our bosses and supervisors. We should be grateful for our jobs and that we live in a country that gives us the right to quit, if we want to; and to go anywhere we want to go. I'm all for improving yourself—working toward your dreams—but wouldn't it sometimes be better if we would just stay put long enough to learn some things, and to help our employers and fellow employees build the kind of organization we say we're looking for?

Take Good Notes

Owners, managers and everyone that is looking for ways to fix problems and improve the organization should *always* keep a pen and paper handy to make notes as you get ideas or see things that need improvement. I can't tell you, as an owner, how frustrating it is to call a meeting to discuss improving the company, and the very people who have been complaining about problems will show up without any written notes of ideas for change. Then they can't remember what needs improving, and they waste valuable time at the meeting.

How to Encourage Yourself

When you are a leader there will be times when no one is around to pat you on the back or to give you a word of encouragement. A leader does not have the option to hold a "pity party." *Your moods won't change things; only actions change things.* Take action over your moods by encouraging yourself with the reading of motivational books, trade journals, and by listening to tapes on successful leaders and organizations in and outside your industry. I suggest reading materials that will help you gain wisdom and knowledge to help fix and eliminate problems in your life and your business. We've all heard the phrase "garbage in, garbage out," and garbage is the thing that sometimes brings discouragement. Well-known motivational speaker, Zig Ziglar calls it "Stinkin' Thinkin'."

Here are some helpful keys to relieve a lot of stress:

- Regular exercise. It makes you feel better and keeps you thinking positive.

- You need to get the right amount of sleep and eat right.

- Limit your association with negative people and associate with people who will give you *wise* counsel.

- Don't run from your problems; *attack* them like you would an enemy. Get out in front of your problems by meeting them before they meet you. That is why this book was written, to help people eliminate and attack problems through a systematic approach. Be pro-active!

You know some people run from their problem by procrastinating and working on things they find easier and more enjoyable, instead of the things they should be working on. These people tend to visit and interrupt others in the building and make personal phone calls instead of working on the task at hand or the problems that need to be fixed. When you ask them later if they have completed a certain task, they will often tell you they didn't have time. *I believe that procrastination is the number one reason that people, businesses and organizations fail.* Failure brings discouragement and discouragement brings more failure.

And David *was greatly distressed;*
for the people spoke of stoning him, because
the soul of all the people was grieved,
every man for his sons and for his daughters:
but David encouraged himself *in the LORD his God*
1 Samuel 30:36

Encouraging Words
The truth of the matter is, building systems is grueling work. Even after ten years of building a great system, we still have some tough days, but those are getting farther and farther apart. Like I tell my employees, "There are so many things going right at Beyer Printing, it's scary!"

One of our front office employees who was concerned we were having a slow month awhile back (and then found out otherwise) said to me, "You know, it just seems so quiet around here anymore, I can really see these systems working!"

As I was working on this book after hours at my office, I received a phone call from a former employee who had recently resigned to take a position at another printing company. To my amazement the first thing he asked was, "Can you tell me why these companies around this town have no system of checks for catching mistakes?" He went on for about five minutes telling me of the chaos in customer service and production at his new job. I will call him Thomas.

I said, "Thomas, it's not that they are stupid or really aren't concerned about the chaos; it's because they just don't know what to do, or where to start."

He said, "I've been trying to tell them how we did it when I was working for you, but no one listens!"

Now, why was this call important enough to tell you about it in this book? Thomas is a fine person and I really like him. We share a lot of the same beliefs. But he was one I had some difficulty with in keeping him on the system. Thomas would tell you now that he has come to appreciate the difference good systems makes. His call to me was another strong confirmation. It works!

The writer of one of our promotions to our customers said it like this: "Beyer Printing has achieved a new standard in print production and service—not only improving production and service, but actually improving itself. This positive feedback loop guarantees that as production and service improves that the system of improvement also improves—creating a system of improvement that is virtually unknown in most businesses." I'm thankful to believe this is not just good press!

Whatsoever things are true, whatsoever things are honest, whatsoever things are just, whatsoever things are pure, whatsoever things are lovely, whatsoever things are of good report; if there be any virtue, and if there be any praise, think on these things.

Phillippians 4:8

Don't Act Great, Be Great!

One of the most disturbing things I see in the business world is the way that companies are constantly looking for new business, while the customers they now have are not receiving anywhere near the service they deserve. They want more and more and when they get more, the customers they have get less.

Have you ever called a company to ask for technical help on a product they've sold you, or to ask them a question about your bill, and they put you on hold for a long time? When you finally get to talk to someone they are often rude or the person is hard to understand and not much help. But if you turn right around and call that same company's *sales* line, they will answer almost immediately with a more receptive person. This is all the evidence you need to see where a company's priorities are. They put a high premium on sales, and not service.

A little hint: When you can't get through for technical help, call the sales line and ask them to put you through to technical help while they stay on the line with you. Tell the sales department about the poor service you are getting. You will be surprised how fast you are taken care of.

How many times have you had telephone companies begging you to switch to their service, and once you sign up, you can't even get them on the phone? And think of the TV commercials that promote a company's "greatness," and then you're disappointed to find they are not great; it was all just great promotions.

My pastor and friend, John Privitt of Calvary Chapel Nashville, says, "Don't act like a Christian, be a Christian!"

The ten years we were building our company's systems, I refused to put the emphasis on sales. I believe that you should be a good steward of what you have and grow step-by-step, but not to the sacrifice of quality and service to your customers.

But he who is greatest among you shall be your servant.
And whoever exalts himself will be humbled,
and he who humbles himself will be exalted.
Matthew 23:11-12

Adam *and* Eve: System Breakdown

According to the Bible, before Adam and Eve sinned, the world and the universe were perfect and complete. All systems worked perfectly, and Adam was happy *keeping* and *dressing* the garden—kind of a hobby and something he enjoyed doing. But after they sinned, and a curse was pronounced on the garden, everything in the universe with all of its systems started breaking down. The earth and things in the earth began to decay, and Adam now had to work the soil with the sweat of his brow. He had to build and maintain his *own* house and food supply.

I think you can relate, if you've ever run a business or an organization. You "sweat" a lot because of system breakdowns that cause chaos. That is why you need great systems that are 100 percent complete. You want to *keep* and *dress* your business; you don't want to sweat. The better the system, the less you sweat!

A View from My Window

A friend of mine wrote the following poem a few years ago, and I was impressed enough to include it in this book because it rang true for me as I worked to bring order to my business and, yes, my personal surroundings.

After the night behind curtain and shade
I look out my window to see what God made
And the sight that I see makes me sad in my heart
I think, "How much better, if all did their part,"
'Cause the things in my view would take little to fix
If each neighbor would bother to straighten and pickup
The rusty old pieces of this and of that

Some towering eyesore, a discarded hat
Toys that a child has not treated with care
Things taken out, not put back, lying there
A garden of tossed paper wrappers and such
Making it right again wouldn't take much
If we each took a moment to think how our ways
Might help out our neighbor and gladden his days
So all that we've worked for is easy to see
Not hidden by refuse and piles of debris
God gave us so much in this beautiful place
Mountains and forests, and smiles for each face
He gave us such wonders as music and light
Colors and rainbows and eagles in flight.
So, today I'll remember to do what I can
To spread love around me, not paper and cans
If the world isn't all that God meant it to be,
Then I'll change what I can, beginning with me

by Susan Meredith, © 2001

CHAPTER 16
THE MYSTERY OF THE CIRCLE
REVEALED

IN THE BEGINNING of this book, I shared about my vision of the circles that, to me, represented systems intersecting and interacting with each other. By now, you understand that the mystery of the circle is *revealed* when you complete the circle and close all the gaps or holes in a system. Then the system will run almost flawlessly. And when you complete all the other circles or system in your organization, so that one system intersects with another system—no gaps—then you have created a well-oiled machine.

It sounds simple and it really is. Everything in the world that seems complex is not hard to understand or build when you break it down into small steps that are like small circles. The hardest part of creating your system will be bringing two or more systems together. Each system in your organization affects every other system. You must bring your people together so, as a team, they can find and fix the holes or gaps. Then the interacting systems won't affect each other in a negative way.

You must also learn to be patient, but persistent, in the creation of your turnkey, closed circuit or complete circle system, which will be *documented* in the operations manual. As you can see it will not happen overnight, it took me over ten years.

It's impossible to imagine how God designed and built so many perfect systems that affect, interact with, and depend on each other! Do you think if He had just waited long enough, they would have designed and built themselves?

More Revelations of the Circle

Here are some of the revelations of what I call the CC Complete Circle, which is a completed system. We will recap and close the circle of this book that, by the way, is also a system.

CC = You only have to build it once and then tweak it from time to time.

CC = Less meetings to stop the chaos, so valuable meeting time can be used to create new systems, if needed, or improve the existing systems, or to creatively brainstorm marketing opportunities for your organization.

CC = Fewer, but more effective managers and assistant managers.

CC = On a scale of one-to-ten of an employees abilities . . . with a good system, a five can become an eight.

CC = Peaceful and happier atmosphere, prompting better employee cooperation and production.

CC = Exposes good and bad employees quickly.

CC = More profit with fewer sales.

CC = More profit with fewer mistakes.

CC = Things don't get lost; so time is saved and money made.

CC = More pride with clean and organized work areas.

CC = Less turnover of customers.

CC = Better service and more respect from vendors.

CC = Attracts highly qualified employees, which in turn attracts other quality employees.

CC = Company or organization is much more valuable as a turnkey operation.

CC = Production speeds up with less effort.

CC = Customers spread, by word of mouth, the good news about the quality and service of the organization. Therefore, less time and money needs to be spent on promoting the organization because of the circle of witnesses promoting your company, free of charge.

CC = Vendors who also sell to your competition, tell their employees about the success of your organization, attracting more and better employees to your company.

CC = More time and resources to give back to your community or non-profit organizations.

CC = Can help your customers better organize their organization, using your system as a model.

CC = Due to the constant transformation of your company, employees are less likely to become complacent or bored.

CC = It is a witness to the employees of your organization, that truth, stewardship, integrity and perseverance will bring honor and success

So, here is how I define CC = Complete Circle:

As you fix the gaps and holes in the circle—you gain more time and profits—which allows you to fix and smooth out even smaller gaps and rough spots in the circle—where you even gain more time and money. And around and around you go until you've created a powerful machine, a great organization, and a valuable *operations manual* for a valuable company.

You own a business; you haven't just created yourself a job.

The mystery of the circle has been revealed.

The LORD by wisdom hath made the earth;
by understanding He created the heavens.
Proverbs 3:19

CLOSING REMARKS

IF YOU HAVE finished reading this book, I want to thank you. I hope you have gleaned some ideas and information that will help you in your business and maybe even your life. Writing this book has been a milestone I will never forget.

As we were doing the final edits of this book two things became abundantly clear to me . . .

1. You or I might build a great turnkey business—one that had systems that would surpass any company on the globe. But a single Act of God could end it all. I must invoke the blessings of God over my business and my life, for without God I know I am nothing.

> *I am the vine, you are the branches:*
> *He that abides in Me, and I in him,*
> *the same brings forth much fruit:*
> *or without Me* you can do nothing.
> *John 15:5*

2. People are your greatest asset and without them the gears of industry would not turn. If I have given the impression in this book that systems can replace people, then I would like to set the record straight. Some systems replace the need for some people, but not the ones who will serve with you in a systematic, cooperative effort to grow your company for the betterment of all concerned.

When a typesetting machine called the Linotype was invented at the turn of the 20th century, it was able to do the work of about six people who, at that time, set type by hand. But the machine still had to have an operator. The Linotype was a great tool for mankind, but no tool or system will ever replace us. The systems that I value and teach in this book are tools to be a blessing to people. No system that I could ever invent or suggest could rival or replace God's most valued creations—you and me.

I will praise thee; for I am fearfully and wonderfully made: marvelous are Thy works; and that my soul knows right well.
Psalms 139:14

I also firmly believe in giving back to your community when you have been blessed. I have practiced this and found the following to be true . . .

Honor the Lord with your possessions
and with the first fruits of all your increase.
So your barns will be filled with plenty and
your vats will overflow with new wine.
Proverbs 3:9-10

Profile of the Ideal Employee

1. Honest with others
2. Honest with self
3. Eager to learn about their trade or position
4. Able to work with others
5. Punctual
6. Clean dress
7. Good work habits

   Goes from one task to the next without getting side-tracked

   Concentrates on the task at hand

   Takes pride in doing quality work

   Keeps work area clean

   Keeps items that they are working with organized

8. Able to take constructive criticism without being defensive
9. Does not point the finger at other workers to cover up their own short comings
10. Does not use foul language out of respect to others
11. Is not intimidated by change
12. Is constantly looking for ways to improve themselves and their work place, not just point out problems
13. Likes to share with others the things they have learned to make other fellow workers' jobs easier
14. Has a willingness to go the extra mile
15. Does not need someone constantly watching them to stay on the system
16. Will not encourage or agree with supervisors or fellow workers in wrong actions, just to gain points or keep the status quo
17. Does not take advantage of stressful situations (that sometimes come upon fellow workers or management) for further advancement or personal gain
18. Does not blame their supervisor for tough decisions they have to make or should make

beyer printing inc.

𝔐𝔦𝔰𝔰𝔦𝔬𝔫 𝔖𝔱𝔞𝔱𝔢𝔪𝔢𝔫𝔱

We are in the business of assisting our customers in meeting their printing and print design needs. To this end, we are committed to providing <u>the most consistent</u> high quality and best customer service in the printing industry.

To assure our customers of our promise of "Master Quality", and GREAT CUSTOMER SERVICE, Beyer Printing employs only quality-minded, well-trained personnel. These assurances will be witnessed in every phase of our business with an emphasis on excellence, prompt service, courtesy, cleanliness, honesty, a genuine concern for our customers, and a **quality control system** that allows nothing to leave our facility that doesn't meet or exceed the expectations of our customers.

Our systems, work ethic, service, willingness to keep up with the latest industry innovations and the offering of unique products will remain our hallmark and our vehicle toward new business.

Through these commitments we build our futures, to the benefit of our company, our customers, ourselves, our children and our children's children for generations to come.

— *The Staff of Beyer Printing*

BEY-GM-016 REV 09/04

beyer printing inc.

Code of Ethics

We commit ourselves to a high standard of excellence in the production of graphic arts, <u>by adhering</u> to a **system of quality control checks** during each phase of manufacturing.

We will not accept work, we are unable to produce that meets or exceed our customers' expectations.

We promise to treat each customer as if they were our ONLY customer.

We promise to charge fairly for all of our products and services - fair for the customer, fair for Beyer Printing and the graphic arts industry.

— The Staff Of Beyer Printing

BEY-GM-017 REV 09/04

Person doing the bustin'   # SYSTEM BUSTER

_____

DATE:_____/_____/_____

Account Name _(if applicable)_:_____   Job Ticket # _(if applicable)_:J_____

Explain situation:

_____

_____

_____

_____

Management will fill out everything below this line

Non Conforming Events

☐ Job Ticket ☐ _Wrong or_ ☐ _Incomplete info_   ☐ Items Out of Place _(Can't Find Something)_
☐ Process Error from Previous Dept.   ☐ Maintenance on equipment not done
☐ Equipment Down or Malfunction   ☐ Interruptions Internal _(UnNecessary)_
☐ Supplies not available _(unscheduled pick)_   ☐ Interruptions from Outside _(UnNecessary)_
☐ Other_____

Persons involved

_____ ☐ Personal Error ☐ System Error
            Name   Department   Signature

_____ ☐ Personal Error ☐ System Error
            Name   Department   Signature

_____ ☐ Personal Error ☐ System Error
            Name   Department   Signature

_____ ☐ Personal Error ☐ System Error
            Name   Department   Signature

■ Personnel Error _(System Not Followed)_   ■ System Error _(Need to correct System)_

Steps taken to <u>correct situation immediately</u>____ _(This is not System Changes)_ :

_____

_____

Is this a ☐ Predictable Event   ☐ Unpredictable Event   ☐ Not Sure

If <u>unpredict able</u> explain why_____cont. on back

If <u>predict able</u> ☐ system changes or ☐ new procedure to be made to prevent reoccurrence

_____

_____

_____cont. on back

Persons who came up with solution _____

☐ Employees trained on new system update

_____
    Department Manager

_____
    General Manager

| Cost: $_____ |
| Time lost _____hrs._____min. |

BEY-PA-333   REV 2/04

FORM CHANGE/UPDATE CHECKLIST

GENERAL MANAGEMENT

STEP 1

- [ ] Paper Clip this form to the form being updated and write its form number in the box on the right
- [ ] Updates or Changes marked with red pen (new form written out clearly)
- [ ] New form printed clearly or typed in Word doc. & emailed to philip@beyerprinting.com

Form Number of form being updated:

_____   _____
Person Requesting Form Update   Date

Place this form, & form with marked changes, in forms box on General Manager's door

STEP 2

- [ ] General Manager has approved Changes (or New Form)

_____
General Manager's Signature

SYSTEM MANAGER:

STEP 3

- [ ] Update Policy & Procedure forms to *Word* PC Only
  (Use Templates found in Form Template Folder in Beyer Forms Management Folder)
- [ ] Material Lists use *Excel*. Checklist, Job Ticket Form, and other forms will stay in *Quark* until further notice.
- [ ] Material Lists that are updated have been updated in PRISM (see codes for Prism)
- [ ] Revision date correct
- [ ] If change related to website, website updated (If Applicable)
- [ ] Master Forms List updated and printed for the front of Department Operation Manual and put in Forms Completed Bag in *Customer Service Dept* (New forms only)
- [ ] The computer file for this form has been filed correctly

Initials

Place this form, form with marked changes, and new updated form in forms box on General Manager's door

STEP 4

- [ ] General Manager has approved art

_____
General Manager's Signature

Place this form, form with marked changes, and new updated form in Forms Completed Box in Customer Service Dept./ Production Administration

PRODUCTION ADMINISTRATION:

STEP 5

- [ ] All old copies of the form being updated have been thrown away (every location)
- [ ] New copies made and placed in designated location
- [ ] New original copy placed inside operation manual and old copy removed
- [ ] Place this form stapled to old form with marked changes in Forms Change Binder

Initials

BEY-GM-009   REV 01/04

Human Resources HR-1000

		Date this sheet was printed		1/11/2005

Form Name	Form No.	Stock Required	Ink Color	Bindery Requirements
Employment Application	HR-1000	20# White Bond	Black	Insert in Orientation Packet
Master Glossary	HR-1001	20# White Bond	Black	GBC Bound
Glossary Addendum	HR-1001A	20# White Bond	Black	Insert in Employee Manual
Employee Manual	HR-1002	20# White Bond	Black	Insert in Employee Manual
History of Printing	HR-1003	20# White Bond	Black	Insert in Employee Manual
Accounting Glossary-NOT SET	HR-1004	20# White Bond	Black	Insert in Employee Manual
Overview Of Printing Terms	HR-1005	20# White Bond	Black	Insert in Employee Manual
See procedures	HR-1006			
Use for new form	HR-1007			
See procedures	HR-1008			
Orientation Checklist for Hir Mgr	HR-1009	20# White Bond	Black	Hiring Mgr Orientation Man.
Orientation Test	HR-1010	20# White Bond	Black	Insert in Orientation Packet
Employee Statement	HR-1011	20# White Bond	Black	Insert in Orientation Packet
Emp Guidelines	HR-1012	20# White Bond	Black	Insert in Employee Manual
New Employee Orientation Chklist	HR-1013	20# White Bond	Black	Insert in Orientation Packet
Profile of Ideal Emp.	HR-1014	20# White Bond	Black	Insert in Orientation Packet
Glossary Test-NOT SET	HR-1015	20# White Bond	Black	None Required
Record of Discipline	HR-1016	20# White Bond	Black	Cut & Pad in 50's
Req. for Sick Pay	HR-1017	20# White Bond	Black	None Required
Request for leave	HR-1018	20# White Bond	Black	None Required
Inj. Rprt.-Govt form	HR-1019	Special	Black	None Required
I-9 Govt Form	HR-1020	Special	Black	None Required
W-4 Govt Form	HR-1021	Special	Black	None Required
Non-Compete Agreement	HR-1022	20# White Bond	Black	None Required
Absenteeism Form	HR-1023	20# White Bond	Black	None Required
Notification of Resignation	HR-1024	20# White Bond	Black	None Required
Use for new form	HR-1025			
Use for new form	HR-1026			
Use for new form	HR-1027	20# White Bond	Black	None Required
New Emp Orientation Envelope List	HR-1028	20# White Bond	Black	None Required
Performance Appraisal (non-exempt)	HR-1029	20# White Bond	Black	None Required
Performance Appraisal (exempt)	HR-1030	20# White Bond	Black	None Required
See policies	HR-1031			
See policies	HR-1032			
See policies	HR-1033			
See policies	HR-1034			
Employee Handbook Receipt	HR-1035	20# White Bond	Black	None Required
Employment Contract	HR-1036	20# White Bond	Black	None Required
See policies	HR-1037			
W-9 Govt Form	HR-1038	20# White Bond	Black	None Required
Quick Application by Telephone	HR-1039	20# White Bond	Black	None Required
Occupational Health Treatment Form	HR-1040	20# White Bond	Black	None Required
See policies	HR-1041			
See procedures	HR-1042			
Sepration Notice State of TN	HR-1043	20# White Bond	Black	None Required
Policies				
Vacation Policy	HR-1031	20# White Bond	Black	None Required
Persl Phone Call, Cell, Policy	HR-1032	20# White Bond	Black	None Required
Checklist Policy	HR-1033	20# White Bond	Black	None Required
Overtime Policy	HR-1034	20# White Bond	Black	None Required
Reprint Due to Error Policy	HR-1037	20# White Bond	Black	None Required
Computer Use and Internet Policy	HR-1041	20# White Bond	Black	None Required
Procedures				
Interview Questions-CSR	HR-1006	20# White Bond	Black	None Required
Interview Questions-Production Appl	HR-1008	20# White Bond	Black	None Required
Performance Appraisals instructions	HR-1042	20# White Bond	Black	None Required

Daily Routine Checklist

- ❏ Computer & printers turned on
- ❏ Log into System100 to check for Special Tasks, Emails and Company Memos (Home Page)
- ❏ Time Sheets picked up and given to Gen Manager
- ❏ Time Sheets place in 3 Ring Binder & kept for 3 weeks
- ❏ Will Call-Call customers ASAP
- ❏ Daily Routine Checklists (All Depa rtments) filed. Employee comments on these sheets emailed to Gen Manager
- ❏ Customer Invoices entered, printed & mailed
- ❏ Invoice pink copy attached to Prism Invoice copy
- ❏ Invoice pink copies put in numerical order and placed in top tray till the end of the month
- ❏ Signed packing & delivery slips are placed in a folder & kept in top tray till the end of the month
- ❏ Customer Invoice yellow copies put in numerical order in the tray till the end of the month
- ❏ Computer backed up (Internally) on Mon. Wed. Fri
- ❏ 2 copies of back up written to disk on Wed. & Fri
  Take one disk home
- ❏ New pickups added to Delivery/Pickup form in System100

2:00

- ❏ Stock PO's (Stock Packing Slips Received bag in warehouse) reviewed due date and checked to see if stock has arrived. If late called vendor
- ❏ Supplies PO's (Stock Packing Slips Received bag in warehouse) reviewed due date and checked to see if stock has arrived. If late called vendor
- ❏ Vendor called if credit invoice not received on stock we have returned. Fax copy of vendor pickup form if necessary
- ❏ Stock & supplies PO's married w/Packing Lists Received and Posted in Prism
- ❏ Inventory sheet GM-013 updated on any incoming Equipment, Hardware, Software, Furniture, etc…
- ❏ Mail opened and filed
- ❏ Customer Payments entered
- ❏ Customer Payments copies given to Production Admin
- ❏ Bank deposit made
- ❏ Vendor Bills entered in accounting software
- ❏ Packing slips attached to Vendor Bills
- ❏ Vendor Bills filed, by date, in Bills Due folders
- ❏ Vendor Bills paid
- ❏ Vendor Bills attached to Check Copy and filed in Paid Bill folder til the end of the month
- ❏ Credit Application (Beyer) faxed to Vendor (If Applicable)
- ❏ Customer Account Aging Report printed
- ❏ Customers called on past due bills and notes made on these calls
- ❏ Aging Report faxed to customer (If Applicable)
- ❏ Aging Invoice faxed (If customer requests)
- ❏ Credit Application received on new customers who request terms. The fir st orde r is C.O.D.
- ❏ References called on Customer Credit Application
- ❏ Customer notified if approved for credit
- ❏ Problem accounts given to General Manager
- ❏ Marketing letters mailed (If Applicable)
- ❏ Copier maintenance scheduled with vendor)

ACCOUNTING/ General Office

- ❏ Supplies reviewed: Supplies needed, ordered in System100 in Accounting/ Bookkeeping Dept. under Inventories
- ❏ Postage stamps purchased (if needed)
- ❏ Employee files/info updated (If Applicab le)
- ❏ Fax Transmittal Sheet Filed Purge sheets ov er 6 months
- ❏ Request for Leave forms checked on email, printed and employee's have signed, then filed and posted on Calendar- System100
- ❏ Vacations & Holidays added to Calendar- System100
- ❏ Absenteeism forms checked on email, printed and Production Admin has signed, then filed
- ❏ Request for Leave & Absenteeism forms posted in System100 (If Applicab le)

Weekly

- ❏ 941 payroll tax deposit payment made (Tuesd ay)
- ❏ Payroll Summary Report for Time Cards printed (Thursda y)
  Produced in Prism Job Costing\ Employee Report\ Start Date-End Date\ Report Type-"Payroll Summary" Print out per employee
- ❏ Payroll Summary Report placed in 3 Binder permanently
- ❏ Payroll Completed (Thursday)
- ❏ Paychecks given to employees (Friday)
  Sales Tax paid before 20th of the month

Monthly

- ❏ Sales Rep's Sales Report given to General Manager
- ❏ P & L Report printed for General Manager
- ❏ Value Ad ded and 100% Ratio report completed, filed and printed. Copy to Gen Mgr.
- ❏ Tracking Char t Ratios from Ratio reports completed and emailed to Prepress for output of poster. Copy to Gen Mgr.
- ❏ System Busters & Rerun Due To Error sheets cost have been added up
- ❏ Backup disk made and taken to CPA
- ❏ Bank Statement reconciled, print copy and file
- ❏ Bank Statement (copy) taken to CPA
- ❏ Loans due paid from Escrow Checking Account
- ❏ Material Usage Report on Heidelberg Plates & Hamada Plates printed for use in Waste Ratio Reports Procedure : (Prism Job Costing\ Reports\ Material Usage\ Category\ Item\ Set Date\ Sort by date)
- ❏ Missing Invoice Report printed
- ❏ Rent paid to escrow account
- ❏ Copier meter reading faxed to R.J. Young

I have checked off and done all of these items on t his to-do list:

X_____

Date: ___/___/___

BEY-AD-201 REV 11/04

Books That Make a Difference

The following is a list of some of the books I highly recommend as you build your business:

The Bible
Scripture references used in this book taken from the King James and the New King James Version © 1982 Thomas Nelson

My Utmost for His Highest
by Oswald Chambers. Discovery House Publishers, © 1963

The E Myth
by Michael Gerber. Harper Business, © 1986

How to Gain an Extra Hour Every Day
by Ray Josephs. Published by Thorsons, © 1992

File, Don't Pile
by Pat Dorff. St. Martin's Press, © 1983

The Goal
by Eliyahu M. Goldratt *and* Jeff Cox. North River Press, © 1984

Taking the Mystery Out of TQM
by Peter Capezio *and* Debra Morehouse. Career Press, © 1993

The One Minute Manager
by Kenneth Blanchard *and* Spencer Johnson. Berkeley Publishing Company, © 1981

Financial Peace

by Dave Ramsey. Lampo Press, © 1992, 1995 and by the Penguin Group, © 1992

The Printer's Chart of Accounts
by Stuart W. Margolis, CPA-PIAS. Printing Industries of America, © 1989.

Delivering Knock Your Socks Off Service
by Ron Zemke and Kristin Anderson. AMACOM, © 1993

No Excuses Management

by T.J. Rodgers. Currency; Book and Diskett edition, © 1993

The 21 Most Powerful Minutes in a Leader's Day

by Dr. John C. Maxwell. Thomas Nelson Publishers, © 2000

About the Author, Philip Paul Beyer

In 1963, Tex Lyons' printing establishment in Baton Rouge, Louisiana, was an unlikely hangout for a 14-year-old, budding entrepreneur. Philip was fascinated with his visits to the print shop and watching his brother William, a new apprentice there, "man the presses." He marveled at the workings of the presses and the whole printing industry. It wasn't long before Tex offered Philip a job collating in the bindery department. To be able to work beside and do like his brother—learning such exciting skills, drinking Cokes all day, and making fifty cents an hour—was an opportunity not to be missed. For Philip Beyer it was also the beginning of a deep appreciation of the printing trade; a life-long calling to a business that had revolutionized the world and changed the very course of history.

Even a short forty years ago, printing was much different than it is today, entering the new millennium. Printing was a craft that found young men working as apprentices for years to learn how to become journeymen printers. Master printers were, and still are, a rare breed. Back then a lot of printing was done on letter presses— slow by today's standards but able to produce high quality results. The *offset press* was fast replacing the letterpress. But the face and pace of the printing trade was changing rapidly. Business people no longer cared so much about "the art of printing" as more and more they needed an almost instant and endless supply of forms and marketing materials to help them run their business more efficiently.

Philip Beyer had entered into this creative industry during one of its most significant changes in half a century. Other higher paying jobs drew young Philip away briefly, but they lacked the sense of satisfaction and craftsmanship he had experienced as a printer. So, he turned back to his "first love," printing. At another firm— Kennedy Print Shop, owned by Carl Williamson, a Linotype operator—Philip learned a lot about the trade that would build the foundation for his future.

After graduating from high school, he took on college studies for a very short while, until the lure of yet another, powerful "love" began to fill every spare thought. He had begun playing music and singing in high school. Music in the late 1960s and early 1970s, was just about every young man's fantasy, and for this particular young man—with the heart of an entrepreneur and a head full of dreams— music became his all-consuming reality! Now, with assurance that he had found his true calling, he left college and worked all the harder as a printer to be able to pursue his music interests, nights and weekends in Louisiana. This new incentive found him operating most of the letter presses around; Klugies, Heidelbergs and even old hand presses. He also made it a point to learn everything he could about offset printing, and all other facets of the printing business; even keeping up with the latest industry trends. But music had become his greatest passion and printing would allow him to afford it.

By 1974, Philip's music was keeping him busy full-time, and although he would not enter the printing trade again for many years, his printing experience was put to good use in promoting his increasingly popular band, Papa Joe and Riverboat, later known as Philip Paul and Patrol (see bandsfromthepast.com). Looking at printing from the other side of the fence was teaching him lessons that would prove invaluable later as he related to his customers.

But the success of Philip's music was the very thing that began to take the greatest toll. After years of heavy performance and rehearsal schedules; late nights in crowded, smoky venues; endless hotels and motels; the incalculable rigors of the road; and—worst of all—missing his family, Philip Paul hung up his microphone.

Philip Beyer learned much from being a performer, bandleader and manager of a touring show—discipline, marketing and promotion. He learned how to take care of business, plan and keep schedules, meet payrolls, manage finances and accounting, and the importance of well-considered tools and equipment. He also learned about people. Relationships—that's where real success begins!

After twenty years on the road, Philip Paul Beyer returned to a lifestyle he had longed for, instilled by Christian parents whose values and ideals were to become the solid basis for all his future endeavors. Philip Beyer is owner and president of Beyer Printing Inc. of Nashville, Tennessee.

INTRODUCTION TO
SYSTEM100

SYSTEM100 IS the application we have created that I mentioned earlier in this book. As I've stated, I spent ten years developing an operations manual to turnkey our printing company. You may remember
me saying that around my seventh year of building our operations
manual, I had my company running so well that I was completely
out of debt and could have gone fishing or learned to play golf really
well. But I really wanted to take these systems and ideas I had discovered to the next level. I wanted to make them public. *System100*
is the next level! It gives our employees direct access to our *operations manual*. Many of our systems are now automated through
System100.

 System100 is a great tool to transform a company into a powerful machine. It will help you download the business systems you
have been carrying around in your head into its database. We are
constantly finding new ways of using *System100* to automate the
way we do business, and it is continually being reviewed and
improved by our company.

 With *System100* you won't have to spend ten years building
your *operations manual* and other systems to transform your company. *System100 will rapidly accelerate that process.*

 Before I commissioned a software company to write *System100*,
I looked throughout the business world for something like it. I
wanted to save myself the time and money I knew it would take to
build it. Trust me, if I could have found it on the market, I would
have bought it without thinking twice.

 If someone one would have offered me *System100* when I first
started on the mission of turning my company into the ultimate organization, I would have thought I had inherited a great fortune.

FEATURES OF *SYSTEM100*

• Web based application run on Windows based server
• Company Intranet
• Password protected
• User privileges
• Administrative privileges
• Department assignment

Departments
Option to change names of departments seen on main dashboard

Repository for Documents
Folders *and* subfolders
Folder-various designs
Files-upload, viewable and printable
    Word
    PDF
    Jpeg
    Links
    Notes

System Buster-Data Base System
This is the leak detector. This system will find every hole or gap in the system
• Auto numbering
• Searchable by its own unique number
• Keyword search

Reports in a Given Period
• Total cost *and* time lost
• System Busters personal errors or system errors
• System Busters with personal errors
• System Busters with system errors

- By person with personal errors
- By department with personal errors
- By department with system errors

Reports on Events in a Given Period
- List of all non-conforming events
- List of all predictable events
- List of all unpredictable events
- List of all changes to system suggested
- List of form numbers and the description of the systems changed
- List of person initiating the System Buster and number of times
- List of the explanations why and the person who initiated the System Buster

Request Label System-Data Base System
Great system to use with the 100 percent cleaning system—every item should be in a labeled container
- Size, style, information, number of labels requested
- Request for a label emailed to person making and distributing labels
- Search by label form number, department or type
- Repository for existing labels categorized by departments
- Viewable-upload PDF or Word documents

Emergency Numbers
These numbers should be available on a moment's notice to every employee
Categorized by: category, name, company, phone, mobile phone

System Override-Data Base System
This system is to be used only in circumstances when there is no time to completely implement the system. This is to be used only by certain supervisors. This is not an exemption from the normal system. When using System Override you have to explain exactly why you overrode the system. The head of the organization will be notified and their signature is required.

•Auto numbering
•Searchable by its own unique number

Reports in a given period
• All overrides
• By person

Shipment Tracking
• Linked directly to UPS, FedEx, etc. websites

Company News & Photo Gallery-Data Base System
This system is great for sharing company news and having company photos accessible to everyone in the organization. Example: company picnics or parties, landmark events like moving or expansion projects, putting in new equipment, celebrity visitors, etc.

The Buck Stops Here
This system is to be used only in extreme cases, when any employee needs to contact the head of the organization—not to make a suggestion but because there is a very serious problem. It may be out of fear of retaliation from another employee or supervisor.

Emails go directly to the top person in the organization. Email can only be changed by the administrator of the system

Inventory System-Data Base System
This is also a place to add materials that can be ordered by various departments or asset inventory such as equipment, furniture etc.
• Material can be categorized by departments and many other
    descriptions with each department seeing only their inventory
• Upload picture option

TQM Suggestions -Data Base System
This system is for gathering suggestions for improving the organization from every employee or even outside building service people. With this access the information can be acted on immediately or added to the task system for company projects.

- Auto numbering
- Searchable by its own unique number
- Suggestions emailed to person managing

Forms Update System-*System to Change the System*-Data Base System

This system is for updating your operations manual and ensures that it stays current
- Auto numbering
- Searchable by its own unique number

Reports in a Given Period
- Form number that was updated and person requesting update
- Search by form number that was updated

Job Ticket Update System-Data Base System

This system is for companies that manufacture or use job tickets in their operation. This is not for every organization and is completely optional.

We use this system to send an update or a change to the people responsible for updating or changing a job ticket's specifications. Everyone in production can have access to this system, thereby peoples ideas for improving this job as it is goes through production, or the next time it is produced, insures the job ticket will be updated.

The reason we found this system so affective, is that someone can't say I forgot to update the ticket or I wrote the change on the outside of the ticket but no one changed the digital information. It is completely traceable. All information is stored in database.
- Auto numbering
- Searchable by its own unique number

Reports in a given period of time
- Job ticket number that was updated and person requesting update
- Search by form number that was updated number

Polling System

• Find out what people really think in organization, as this system is completely anonymous
• Set up as many polls as you want
• Option to name the poll
• Option to name and ask as many questions as needed

Company Wide Calendar

This system is for posting employees vacation time and other special events.
• Public and private events

Email System

Designed to be very simple system that is *totally internal.*

All production people can have access without the fear of external problems such as viruses, access to Internet, downloading files and sending or receiving outside email.

Projects and Tasks System-Data Base System

This system is for posting projects and tasks. We even use this for the person that programs *System100* to post improvements to the system we want to implement.
• *Categorized by:*
    Category
    Subject
    Priority
    User
    Assigned to
    Department
    Date
    Status: complete, in progress, deferred, etc.

Company Memo System

You can set up memos that look great with different fonts, sizes and colors

Message Board

Employees can post messages on various topics

Company Links

Self Help Tips Repository-Company Wide

Add tips in document form or links to web sites

Preventive Maintenance System-Data Base System

This system is for tracking and insuring that all preventive maintenance is being documented
• Build custom maintenance checklist with this system
• Auto numbering
• Searchable by its own unique number

Reports on Total Cost and Time in a Given Period

• Routine preventative maintenance
• Total time associated with a person on scheduled preventative maintenance
• Total time associated with a department on scheduled preventative maintenance
•List of routine preventative maintenance checklist form number and form description and number of times completed
•List of routine preventative maintenance checklist and number of times completed associated with the person performing the checklist

Repair Request System-Data Base System

This system is for tracking all repairs made to equipment, building, etc. This also empowers everyone in the organization to request repair on any piece of equipment they are operating—anything from a computer or printing press to a paper shredder, etc.
• Auto numbering
• Searchable by its own unique number
• Keyword search in part description in document
• Part Number search in part description in document

Reports in a given period
• Total cost and time on repairs
• Total cost and time associated with a person doing repair
• Total cost of parts for repair
• Total cost of labor for repair
• Total cost of parts and labor

Reprocess Due to Error System-Data
Base System

This system is for tracking the remaking of a product, in our case reprinting a job. It can be used for any company that is manufacturing a product. This is almost identical to the System Buster system. The reason we have separated it, is for benchmarking purposes, as we can track just those jobs that have to be completely remanufactured.
• Auto numbering
• Searchable by its own unique number

Reports in a Given Period
• Total cost and time lost
• All reprint due to error, personal error or system error
• All reprint due to error with personal errors
• All reprint due to error with system errors
• By person with personal error
• By department with personal error
• By department with system error

List of reasons for reprint
• List of where the error was caught
• List of customer response to the error
• List of all predictable events and number of times they occurred
• List of all unpredictable events and number of times they occurred
• List of all changes to system suggested and number of changes

Absenteeism System-Data Base System

This is filled out by the employee if they have been absent or late. This is a great tool for tracking the person who is chronically late. This absenteeism form is emailed to the person administrating absenteeism.
• Auto numbering
• Searchable by its own unique number
• Key Word Search

Reports in Given Period
• Total number of days absent by employee
• Total number of days absent by all employees
• Total number of times late by employee

Delivery and Pickup System-Data Base System

Any one can assign a delivery and pickup to this list from their workstation. The delivery personnel can print out their own list when they return from a pickup or delivery and don't have to report to various people about next assignment.
• Auto numbering
• Searchable by its own unique number

Bill of Lading System-Data Base System
• Auto numbering
• Searchable by its own unique number
• Search by:
    Date range
    Job #
    Person who filled-out bill of lading
    Consignee (Ship To)
• Drop down list and auto fill
    Freight Companies
    Customers
    Person filling out bill of lading

Skid Flags System
Creates skid flags (Addresses) for shipping skids
• Links to company's shipping module

Proof Correction System-Data Base System
This system is an automated tracking system for proofing of documents between customer, customer service representatives and pre press department. This system insures that all correction are made and documented. This also insures the company is getting paid for the time it takes to make these changes.
• Auto numbering
• Searchable by its own unique number

Proof Shipping System-Data Base System
• Auto numbering
• Searchable by its own unique number

For more information on System100
Beyer Printing, Inc.
1857 Air Lane Drive
Nashville, TN 37210
info@beyerprinting.com

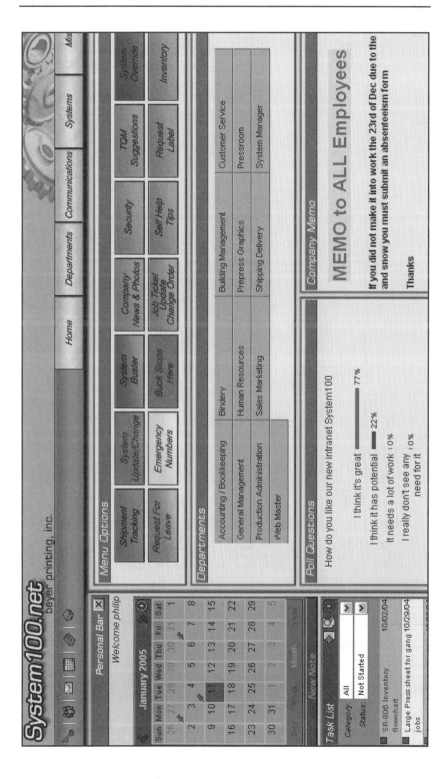

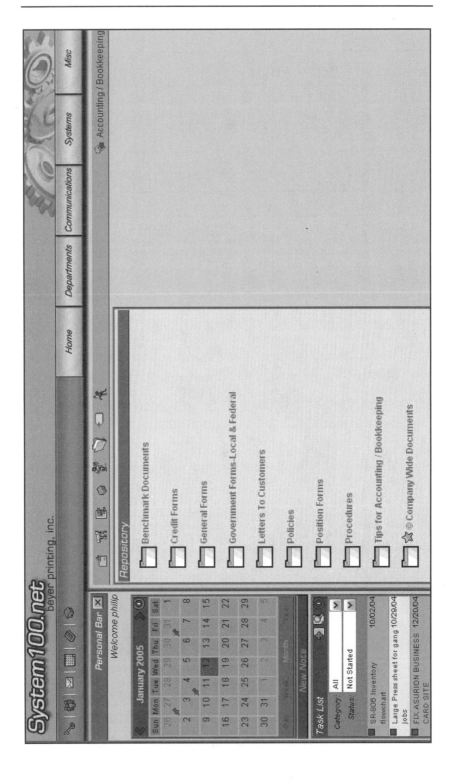

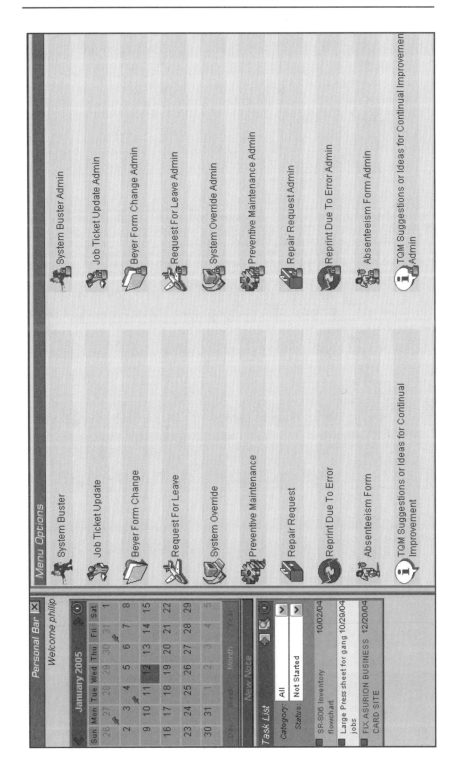

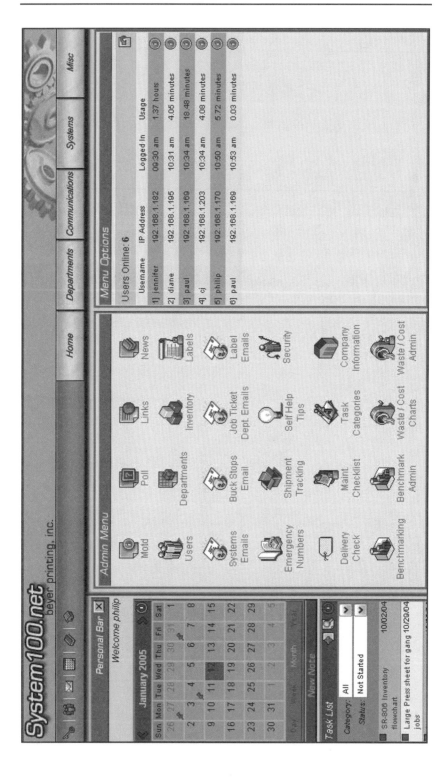

Personal Bar [X]

Welcome philip

January 2005

Sun	Mon	Tue	Wed	Thu	Fri	Sat
26	27	28	29	30	31	1
2	3	4	5	6	7	8
9	10	11	12	13	14	15
16	17	18	19	20	21	22
23	24	25	26	27	28	29
30	31	1	2	3	4	5

Day   Week   Month   Year

New Note

Task List
Category: All
Status: Not Started

SR-806 Inventory flowchart   10/02/04
Large Press sheet for gang jobs   10/29/04
FIX ASURION BUSINESS CARD SITE   12/20/04

Daily Routine Checklist

DELIVERY & PICK-UP

Name of Driver: Jensen, Matt

Truck Number:

Date: 01/12/2005   No: 277

☑ **Clock in** Prism for the day
☑ Distribute supplies received
☑ Pickup up cell phone
☑ Todays Starting Van Mileage 133306

VAN MAINTENANCE

☐ Gas $
☐ Oil Change   Mileage at change
☐ Check oil
☐ Washed & Inside clean and free of debris
Mechanical Problems ○ No ○ Yes
☐ Other
☐ Tags to be renewed in September

DRIVER NOTES:
(Suspected mechanical problems, if any)

Beyer Printing 391-3303

	Pick-Up	Delivery	Completed	Destination	Description
	☑	☐	☐	**ABC Company** 50 Century Blvd Nashville, TN 37214	Artwork @ front desk, when Jennifer is notified
	☑	☐	☐	**Any Company** 1045 Firestone Pkwy LaVergne, TN 37086	film at front counter
	☑		☑	Dennis Paper Company 910 Acorn Drive Nashville, TN 37210	2000 Cougar A-6 white envelopes

NOTES

NOTES

NOTES